Break Through
Featuring
Jonathan Long

Break Through Featuring Jonathan Long

Powerful Stories from Global Authorities That Are Guaranteed to Equip Anyone for Real Life Breakthrough

Jonathan Long

Johnny Wimbrey

Nik Halik

Les Brown

and other leading authorities

WIMBREY TRAINING SYSTEMS
SOUTHLAKE, TEXAS

Copyright © 2018 by Wimbrey Training Systems

Published by
Wimbrey Training Systems
550 Reserve Street, Suite 190
Southlake, Texas 76092

Printed in the United States of America

ISBN: 978-1-938620-42-3

Cover Design by Chris Flynn, Flynn Creative
www.FlynnCreative.com

ARE YOU AN OVERCOMER?

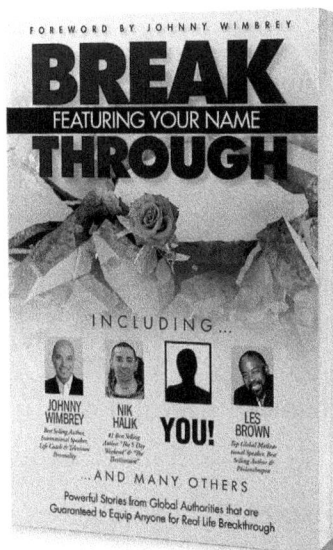

TABLE OF CONTENTS

Foreword

Think back to the hardest, darkest times in your life. What were you going through? How many times did you fail? How did you break through the difficulties and barriers you faced? How did you finally reach the success you knew you deserved?

Why do I ask this? Why do I care about the bad times and failures in your life? I care because how you handled the bad times tell me what type of person you are. I care because the choices you make when you face failure and the lessons you learn as you break through define you.

I can feel your skepticism. You think, really? Failure's important? Why?

Well, I know this to be true. I have had failures and troubles, and my choices turned me into the man I am today. I managed to break past and break through those times.

This is true, too, with the amazing group of authors I have asked to join me in *Break Through*.

I am honored to be joined by the men and women who have made deliberate sacrifices to contribute chapters to this book. Les Brown, Nik Halik, and every one of our other authors will inspire you with their stories of how they broke through their failures and barriers.

All had pain, rejection, and setbacks, and all were able to assess where they were and to make the necessary choices. Every author honestly shares their mistakes and successes with us.

Our *Break Through* authors are brave and fascinating, full of faith in their futures, and generous with their truths. They will help you navigate the crossroads you encounter and help you make sure your choices send you down the path of empowerment, confidence, and success. I am confident they will help you on your journey.

I introduce you now to my *Break Through* partners. Each one is someone I am proud to call a co-author and friend.

—**Johnny Wimbrey**

CHAPTER ONE

Inspect
What You Expect

Johnny Wimbrey

There are many things upon which I am not an authority, and there are many areas in which I will never be able to claim to be an expert, but I can tell you with total confidence that I *am* the authority on the expectation of success.

Every day, I wake up with the expectation for another level of success. I *expect* to find success mentally, emotionally, spiritually, financially, with love, with compassion, and with sensitivity.

I know I will have more of everything that matters to me, and it's just not material things. I crave and expect more knowledge, more honesty, and more good people in my life. My expectation is not arrogant, it's not greedy. My expectation is an intrinsic part of me, and I have honed it and practiced it since I was eighteen years old.

I am Johnny Wimbrey. I am a public speaker and entrepreneur, known around the world for inspiring people and helping them to change their lives. I have built a wonderful life with my wife and children. Now I'm in the privileged position of being able to give back to my community and around the globe.

No one, myself included, would have expected this—let alone predicted it—based on who I used to be. The choices I made, however, made me the man I am today.

Rejection framed my young life. My earliest memory is being hungry in a shelter for battered women. I was three years old and wanted some milk that I found when I opened the refrigerator door. Someone slammed the door on my fingers and told me the refrigerator wasn't ours and the milk wasn't mine to drink because it belonged to another family at the shelter.

That was probably the moment I grasped the unhappy facts: Yes, my mother had left my abusive, alcoholic father; we were temporary guests in a battered women's shelter; my two older brothers and I were homeless.

That feeling of rejection became the mainstay of my childhood and adolescence. My brothers, mother, and I had fled from Texas to California and I didn't see my father for years. I thought he rejected us.

My mother sent us back to live with him a few years later, and I didn't see her for the next three years of my life. More rejection. It was better to think she was dead than she had rejected us. I spent my elementary school years with my unpredictable, alcoholic father who was always busy, doing my best to keep up with my two big brothers: one a future felon, the other a future minister.

I didn't ask to move to California; I didn't ask to be sent back away from my mother, I definitely didn't ask to live with my father again. Looking back, though, I'm so glad I did live with him during those formative years. He gave me the basis for my understanding of expectation.

My father worked as a trash collector for the city. He didn't work in our poor neighborhood; his route took him over to the other side of town, the *rich* side of town. Every year when we had the long Christmas school holiday, my dad took us three boys along after work.

My father wanted us to see what else was out there in the world. He wanted us to see all the things we could have. He pushed us to open our eyes to the innumerable possibilities we had in front of us. Those trips taught me to despise the word *average*. My father raised my expectations. Not then, but later in my adolescence, I took it upon myself to rise to the challenge.

My own expectation for daily increase comes from a garbage man who refused to allow me to accept "average." He taught me to train my vision.

It took me a while to perfect this vision. It was focused on the wrong things in high school, when I made some of the worse decisions of my life. Unfortunately, my focus involved cigarettes, alcohol, drugs, and guns. My teachers told me they saw potential and talent in me and I ignored them. Who were they to tell me how to run my life? I was barreling down a one-way path headed to gang violence, substance abuse, prison, and a literal dead end.

When I was eighteen years old and a junior in high school, my path took a sudden turn when my good friend Mookie was killed by a rival. I went to Mookie's wake to say goodbye, and my brain was teeming with thoughts of death, grief, anger, and vengeance. I packed my gun as I got dressed that evening. I was looking for revenge, ready for a fight, with no glimmer of consequences or the future in my thoughts.

Brooding in my pew, I was barely listening to the speakers until Mookie's mother got up. I knew her, so I gave her the courtesy of listening to her fully. She talked with grace about my dear friend, her son, expressing not only her pain for his loss but actual forgiveness. She stood in front of Mookie's friends, family, and community and forgave her son's murderer. There was no room for interpretation:

"I forgive the man who shot my son."

She could have easily given in to her own anger and thoughts of revenge. She could have lashed out at those who loved her or withdrawn from her life altogether. But she didn't. If Mookie's *own mother*, the woman who loved him more than anyone else on this earth did, could forgive, what right did *I* have to seek vengeance?

A switch went on in my brain. I *knew* this moment was going to change my life. I knew my sudden awareness came straight from God. I was sitting there, conscious and aware, and I heard it clearly, just as if He had leaned over and whispered it directly into my ear: *This will change your life.*

I didn't hear Him because I was better or smarter than everyone around me; I was just ready to listen. God's message was flowing over everyone who was sitting with me; I was tuned to "receive."

I leaned forward and looked up and down the pew. My friends were radiating energy and anger. I could almost see the waves of vengeance coming off their bodies. Two seconds earlier, I was just like them. No more. The moment I changed, sitting there in the pew at Mookie's wake, I knew I expected more than I had the moment before.

My body stilled and I started breathing deeply. If I could have seen into the future, I would have known that every one of Mookie's and my friends would get long-term prison sentences. Perhaps I already did know this.

I knew we had been headed down the same path to the

same dead end. I knew I could have more than this. *I could be more than this.*

After everyone said their "peace" and we were milling around outside, I pulled Reverend Fitzgerald aside.

"Can I talk to you for a second?"

"Of course, son. What is it?"

"I want to give you my gun. If I give you my gun, I know I won't do anything crazy. Reverend, please take it. I don't want to live like this anymore. I am serious this time."

"You know if you give this to me, I'm not going to give it back."

"Yes, sir."

That was it. I gave him my gun. I stopped selling drugs. I stopped breaking the law. I just stopped. The next day I met Crystal, who became my wife a few years later.

I walked away from the life I had been leading. I said I was changing. And I did.

I was blessed with the chance to take what I had been given and use it to climb up and out. My prayers, my conversations with God, and the knowledge that He would give me what I needed when I needed it most, helped me every step of the way. My accomplishments didn't just belong to me; I knew I was being watched and constantly assisted. Instead of giving me complacency, my knowledge that I was never completely alone gave me both comfort and the confidence I needed to take matters into my own hands.

I began to inspect, what I expect.

It saddens me that people feel guilty for expecting more. Why is this the case? Why do they feel uncomfortable if they *expect* more success? Why do they dial back on that verb and replace it with a less aggressive one like "hope?"

The meaning completely changes when you *hope* for more success, or *hope* for better health, or *hope* to improve your financial situation. You give up all involvement and responsibility. You just give up.

There are times when hope has a place in your life and your spiritual and mental process. One never wants to lose hope for your child's continued happiness in life or hope for world peace.

There is a place for hope.

When it comes to your success and things over which you can or could have input and control, you need to **expect**.

My expectations are the basis of my success. Despite the hardships in my life, I can honestly tell you with unwavering confidence I have *never* just been satisfied with what I have so far.

I wake up every day expecting success.

I wish this were an audio book so you could hear the passion in my voice in the words that you are reading right now: I have never entertained a lifestyle of decrease; I have never thought to myself, "this is it." You absolutely, without question deserve your achievements and there is nothing wrong with waking up every day expecting exactly that!

Sashin Governor is a prime example of someone who internalized the concept of expectation at a young age. He accompanied his father to my seminars before he was a teenager, and he was not a shy, self-conscious 12-year old. Sashin sat up front and gave me every ounce of his attention. He put my teachings to work as soon as he was able and hit his first million by the time he was 20. Now, at 23, he is a multimillionaire and speaks on stages around the world.

As he was getting started, he called me almost every day. He never had a little voice in the back of his head that told him that he was bothering me, that it was too many phone calls, that he needed to dial it back. I recognized his hunger and mindset and I gave him direct access whenever he wanted.

Sashin was very young when he heard the concept *expectation to increase*. He was not jaded or tired; he hadn't grown up with limitations on his future. He knew that if he focused on limitation, that's what he would get.

He works like he is broke, every day, and he never stops to count his successes or rest on his laurels. Because he internalizes his expectation to increase, he's growing exponentially, and he'll have his first million-dollar year within two years.

There is so much power in *expectation*. Getting you to the mindset of expecting results will catapult you into a life that most people only dream of having. I want you to get to the mindset and determination of success in the exact same way that when you take a breath you *expect* oxygen, the exact same way that you *expect* a chair to hold you up when you sit down, the exact same way you *expect* the electricity to work when you turn on the lights.

You need to have that exact same expectation for personal triumph. Every day of your life you should wake up with an expectation of success.

It can start for you now. Inspect what you expect! Everyday, *expect* increase and I promise you, *your personal Break Through is imminent!*

Biography

Johnny Wimbrey is a speaker, author, trainer, and motivator, working with sales teams, high-profile athletes, politicians, and personalities around the world.

He has launched three companies—Wimbrey Training Systems, Wimbrey Global, and Royal Success Club International—and heads a sales team of thousands in more than 50 countries, overseeing an active customer database of half a million families.

Johnny shares his powerful message through speaking engagements around the world. He also has a wide media following and has appeared as a guest expert and panelist on television shows including the *Steve Harvey Show, E! News,* and *The Today Show.*

Johnny's first book, *From the Hood to Doing Good,* has sold more than 200,000 copies in printed and digital editions.

Johnny has collaborated on several other books including *Conversations of Success* and *Multiple Streams of Determination;* combined, they have more than 500,000 copies in print.

Johnny regularly speaks for non-profit organizations and reunites children with their families from whom they've been separated for years due to government action. He and his wife, Crystal, are co-founders of Wimbrey WorldWide Ministries, a non-profit which has built six schools in Central America and helped fund water purification systems in Africa.

Contact Information:

Johnny D. Wimbrey
Master Motivation/Success Trainer

MEMBER

NATIONAL SPEAKERS ASSOCIATION

Most Requested Topics:
Motivation/Keynote
Overcoming Adversity
Youth Enrichment
Leadership/Sales

www.johnnywimbrey.com

 @Wimbrey

 @Wimbrey

 @Wimbrey

 JohnnyWimbrey

 @Wimbrey

 LinkedIn@Wimbrey

CHAPTER TWO

Eight Practices of Effective Power Couples

Troy & Angel Mock

"I just don't know, Angel."

Troy looked up from his phone at me as I took another sip of my shake. I didn't want to argue with him—but I knew in my bones I was right.

"Troy, I don't know that I can let this go. Everything about this feels right to me."

It was 2013, and our friend Paul had invited us to join his next business venture again, and even though we both trusted Paul (to be honest, Paul had never been wrong about a business opportunity before), we were already neck-deep in running our construction company. The last thing we needed was another thing on our plate.

But here it was a year later, and when Paul told us he wanted me to at least try the product before we said no again, I knew we owed him that much as his friends.

I t's not every day that opportunity comes knocking twice, but we were lucky enough that it did. Once I tried it, a switch flipped for me, and my gut was telling me that *this was it.*

The only problem was Troy wasn't there yet.

Even though he had doubts, though, there was something about this company that was *different*, and something inside of me couldn't let another year slip by before I dug into this new opportunity. (Besides, I hadn't felt this good in years.)

The conversations that followed could have gone a lot of different ways. Troy could have decided he wasn't interested and continued with the construction business. I could have ignored my instincts, and I could have kept doing what I was doing.

Instead, we leveled the playing field and chose to listen to each other. Like we have since the day we got married, we chose to trust each other. And at the end of the day, we had our closest friends at our kitchen table sharing with them our chance to change everything—together.

Power couples aren't born— they're made.

So how did we do it? How did we know what the right choice to make was?

Besides having a firm level of trust, without which we wouldn't be able to have a successful marriage let alone a business, *we have ground rules.*

Twenty-two years and multiple businesses have given us deep insight and the crucial knowledge of how to strategically work with each other. We have learned over the course of these years that our success can be attributed to our ability to capitalize on both our strengths and weaknesses. They say opposites attract, and that definitely applies to our relationship, both personally and professionally. These opposites have also been able to attract a broader range of prospects and opportunities to our business.

Why? People tend to relate to those who are most like themselves. Either they can see a part of themselves or they see who they would like to become within that other person—and if you're one part of a power couple, that means you're twice as likely to find people you can relate to on that level.

As a couple, we each have our own specific groups that relate to one another. We have learned we can also offer a different perspective to those that may not have originally been compelled to work with us as individuals.

Additionally, for us to have made a huge call like that to pursue one business opportunity over another, we had to trust each other on a deep level. Over the years, we have come to understand that we must trust each other's instincts, even when it doesn't always make sense in the moment. We must trust each other as partners in both life and business.

From finding ways to fight fair to establishing ground rules at home, these are the principles we come back to repeatedly as we grow as partners in all facets of our lives.

Even as this team effort has given us an advantage over other entrepreneurs, it also means we find ourselves in predicaments other couples will never have to go through. Just like with any partnership, there are times of disagreement. This is what will make or break a business—or marriage!

The choice is about how much do you listen, how much do you trust, and, if needed, can you put your ego to the side and think with your head not your emotions? Can you look at the situation and analyze from a business perspective instead of an emotional perspective? Partnerships whether married or business can work synergistically! Many business partnerships have built amazing companies. There are fewer success stories of couples who have succeeded. Why?

For couples to succeed—we believe there need to be specific rules in place for you both to live by:

1. Always listen.
2. Never react emotionally.
3. Trust your instinct.
4. Do not let EGO overtake you.
5. Trust your partner—they have both of your best interest at heart.
6. Act in your circle of influence.
7. Build up your partner.
8. Your marriage always comes first.

Always listen

In most relationships, there is usually one talker and one listener. Be careful not to pigeon hole yourself as either!

The talker tends to be the first to give their opinion. A lot of times, they have already made up their minds and are there to convince the listener of why the listener should see it their way. Meanwhile, the listener is taking it all in and can at times be persuaded by said talker. Over time, that persuasion can build resentment. The talker has great intentions but the listener has an opinion as well and it needs to be heard. This can breakdown communication and lead to a breakdown in ultimate decision making. Make sure both listen and both talk.

To make sure everyone is getting their needs met, we recommend taking the Myers-Briggs Type Indicator® personality assessment. The test will give you a better idea of what each of you needs to recharge and help you connect with your prospects on a deeper level.

If you really want to take your partnership to the next level, invest in the CliftonStrengths® assessment test as well. By identifying strengths that you previously might not have been able to name, you'll be able to build each other up, build your team up, and grow as a person yourself.

Never react emotionally

We are human beings with life experiences. These life experiences can affect us in different ways. Some react to situations or decisions in a matter-of-fact manner and others react in an emotional manner. Emotions are what make us who we are and, in most cases, help guide us in the direction we have chosen for ourselves.

In business, however, the emotions handled incorrectly can and will impact you personally and professionally. You must know when emotions can be used to your advantage, such as you have met someone who seems promising to your business. You are excited to work with them because they have displayed attributes you believe would benefit not only you but also them. Emotions to steer clear from usually come in the form of someone who may not agree with you and may become confrontational. Our initial knee jerk reaction is to immediately respond. You MUST use your head and not react!

There is a reason so much relationship advice says you should sleep on it. If you can walk away from something and give it enough space until you can calm down, you are going to make more rational, more reliable decisions.

Trust your instincts

Your instincts will never steer you wrong. I have heard this my entire life. Trust your gut instincts. Your partner may not see it the same as you, but you must stay strong. Stay confident. Stay true to yourself and DO NOT WAIVER. Your partner will sense if your intention is for all the right reasons and not self-benefiting.

Even if the two of you do not agree, if you have a strong gut instinct, you need to follow it. Whether it's a red flag going off or a bright shining beacon telling you to take a step in that direction, and don't ignore those little signs from the universe that you're moving in the direction of your dreams.

Keep ego out of it

Our decisions can sometimes be influenced by our ego. Yes, we all have one. Our desire to be better, to win, to stand out, to be the best. This can and sometimes does impact your decisions. When in a partnership, especially a married partnership, one usually feels the responsibility to be the bread winner. The person who is to bring home all the bacon! With that said, a person's EGO can influence their decisions and also try to influence the decisions of their partner. Be careful not to let that happen. If your partnership is balanced—the other partner will sense (gut instinct again) it and stop it!

Letting your ego get in the way is the fastest way to anger your partner. It's also the fastest way for the both of you to end up upset and at each other's throats. Someone who is good at business always focuses on other people. They may be growing their team, they may be working with you, but you always know that they have someone else's heart at the center of their choices. Make sure you are doing them the same favor.

Trust your partner

Trust your partner—he or she has both of your best interests at heart. At the end of the day, you entered your partnership for many reasons. Those reasons are what you draw upon to make your final decisions knowing there is trust and admiration for the other person. These reasons also are why your partnership will or will not eventually work. The more you work together, the more you will understand each other's thoughts, reactions, and responses. You will continue to see their integrity, their commitment to you and your cause, their style in which they handle each situation. In turn, you will build trust.

Again, you decided this partnership for a reason. The two of you have something shared that deserves to be cherished.

Circle of influence

You are an individual. You have unique desires, wants, and needs. You have specific ways of showing up in the world that are unique to you. And no matter how much you and your partner might have in common, your biggest strengths lie in capitalizing on your differences.

When it comes to your preferences regarding food, fitness, finances, and more, there is opportunity to create your own space in your relationship and your business. Especially if your business relies heavily on building a team—and whose doesn't?

Your ability to expand your network in separate directions within each person's circle of influence is vital to the long-term health of your business and partnership.

With so many chances to grow and maintain your individuality, this is one way you can reduce the risk of getting sick of each other. Because let's face it, every partnership is found to have its ups and downs.

You control you

As in life, things will happen. You must learn to improvise, adapt, and overcome. Life happens. What separates the winners from the losers is your ability to adapt quickly.

Before you get upset about something, ask yourself, "What do I have control over here?"

The only consistent answer across-the-board is *how you react.* Whether that is any situation with your partner or addressing fires as they flare up in your business, the only thing you can control 100 percent of the time is you. Take responsibility for yourself - and then take action.

Build up each other

Taking the time to actively build each other up is an important trait of successful marriages and businesses. Don't take your partner for granted! It's too easy and it quickly becomes a slippery slope for other things as well.

Your positive attitude whether it's your team listening or your partner, you have the ability to influence those around you for the better. Don't take that responsibility lightly.

Marriage always comes first

As much fun as making money as a couple is, there is no amount of money that matters as much as the two of you making it work.

Not every couple can work together. And that is just fine! What's important is for you both to understand each other, respect the way the other feels, and find ways you can work together regardless of your differences.

Completely possible

Being a power couple is no easy feat—but we wouldn't run our business any other way. With continued commitment to your partnership and dedication to making your business work, it's completely possible to have a successful marriage and business at the same time.

Biography

Troy & Angel Mock are 22-year industry veterans and multi-million-dollar earners in the direct sales industry. Together, their organizational totals surpass 800,000 distributors/customers producing more than $200 million in combined organizational sales globally.

In addition to direct sales, they started and built up a successful construction business serving thousands of customers in Dallas-Ft. Worth, Houston, Austin, and Oklahoma City with thousands of customers.

They have two children, are very family oriented and currently reside in the Dallas-Ft.Worth area.

Contact Information:

Facebook & Instagram: @TroyMockThrives
Facebook & Instagram: @AngelMockThrives
Website: www.TroyAndAngel.com
Email: TroyAndAngelThrive@gmail.com

CHAPTER THREE

Obsessed with Money

Chelsea Galicia

I am obsessed *with* money. Personal and business finance, the economy, investing, and money in politics consume most of my working hours.

Don't misunderstand me, please. I am not obsessed *over* money. That's a very different path—a dangerous path—to take. Money alone can never make you happy, and I learned this truth the hard way.

By the time I was born, my parents' rags-to-riches story was well past the raggedy part. My mom had encouraged my dad to open up his own law firm in Los Angeles, and during my early childhood he grew his business while my mom worked and went to school part time.

When I was 10, my mom graduated from college with a degree in business administration and accounting. As soon as she passed the CPA exam, she went to work at my dad's law firm.

By this time, we lived quite comfortably and were looked after by a rotating staff of fulltime housekeepers in a home that my cousin called the pink White House. There would be other homes too—one that we stayed in every other summer for our vacations on Maui, one in the local mountains for skiing, one by the beach, and another on a golf course in the desert.

My mom felt it was important for my sister and me to understand where she came from—a dirt-floor home in Guaymas, a Mexican fishing village. Every year, my family would make the 16-hour drive so that we could give out used clothes, shoes, and toys to the people of the poor town where my grandfather lived.

My parents wanted us to understand what life was like for many people on the planet and to appreciate what we have. It worked—maybe a little too well. I took it to a level that probably no one intended. Yes, I felt grateful for my indoor toilet (just across from my very own Jacuzzi bathtub), but I also felt guilt for having so much when others had so little. Why was I so lucky? What had I done to deserve the good life that I had been born into?

The only honest answer was a whole lotta nothing. The only way I could reconcile my unearned good fortune was to live a life that honored my parents and helped others. So I saw it as my obligation to do well in school—that was important to my parents—and to show others and myself that I did not take my blessings for granted.

I did well in school, even though I hated every minute of it. And I did well in gymnastics, too; even though I loathed many minutes of it, because my parents liked that I did gymnastics. And as for career plans, I would honor my parent's work and legacy by becoming a lawyer and one day taking over the law firm they had built. In making this suggestion for my life, my mom explained that only a lawyer could own a law firm and so if no one in the family was a lawyer and something happened to my dad, we'd be forced to sell the firm. And, for dramatic effect, she added a white lie: "And we would lose everything." So with that, and a condo in Hollywood to live in, I was off to law school.

Until I passed the bar, I worked summers and part-time at my dad's firm doing depositions (questioning of witnesses under oath). As soon as I took the bar exam, I went full-time and shortly thereafter was given my first caseload, though I still didn't know if I had passed. (I did!)

Everything was looking good. I was a licensed attorney going to court, taking depositions, managing a caseload, and settling cases. The plan seemed to be on track. But soon enough, I couldn't shake the feeling that something was not right, that this was not right for me.

Part of the reason that this work had appealed to me, aside from honoring my parents, was that the work itself was honorable. I would be fighting for the little guy, an injured worker, against the big, bad insurance company who was denying him (or her) financial support and medical care needed to recover from an injury. The reality was disappointing, though not because most people are faking an injury. That kind of fraud happens less often than most people believe.

The real disappointment was with the legal and medical system. The kind of medical treatment people were getting was unhelpful at best, dangerous at worst. People were being pumped full of pain medication and under treatment regimens that seemed to benefit the doctors and pharmaceutical companies more than the patient.

I was furious with doctors and insurance companies for denying or delaying medical treatment, which prolonged pain and suffering, and sometimes required more invasive procedures than if the condition had just been treated right away.

I would be livid at how defense attorneys were incentivized by their compensation structure to drag out cases and create long drawn out battles when they were completely unnecessary.

The judicial system disappointed me, too. Sometimes a judge would be lazy and simply refuse to move forward with trial on the day it was set for, after all the work and waiting.

Then the compensation was often indefensibly, ridiculously small. After all the disastrous medical treatment and outcomes, the years of battles with the insurance company, the dismal compensation that people would get for life-altering injuries was just absurd, and it was my job to tell clients that this was all that they were entitled to under the system.

On top of that, I knew that my clients were in no position to handle the tens of thousands of dollars that they would be receiving in a lump sum. Mix human nature, my clients' level of education, and their often dire circumstances into this mess, and you can bet they'd run through their entire settlement in no time, making the whole massive effort an exercise in futility.

I wasn't really helping these people in any meaningful way, and there was no way I could make a real difference in their lives in my capacity as their lawyer. The system was broken. It was slowly beginning to dawn on me that this work was sucking up my energy and my sense of meaning.

When I looked ahead, I saw this would be my life from here on out. I had worked so hard in high school, college, and law school to get here. My parents had spent so much money on my education and supporting me for 25 years until I finally fulfilled their dream and became a lawyer.

When I took over the law firm, my parents could take more time off and ultimately enjoy retirement, as they had left their crowning achievement in the hands of the daughter they had so meticulously groomed. This was how I would support myself and sustain the high standard of living that had come to feel normal. This is how I'd be part of a rags-to-riches story, because I certainly didn't have one of my own.

To make matters worse, I began to realize that my dad, who for most of my life had been like my best friend, was not the man I had believed he was. I am grateful to my father for the immense support, financial and otherwise, that he provided me growing up, but for reasons I will keep to myself, I lost respect for him.

In short, he had become the epitome of the stereotype that gives lawyers their bad rap. Money had become everything to him. I do not mean to imply here that I discovered illegal activity on his part; I'm talking about his values and how he treated others. He wasn't truly happy, and he was taking it out on people around him.

And then he filed for divorce after 26 years of marriage; now there was no family or family business that I needed to protect.

All signs pointed to me getting out. The voice in my head repeatedly said, "This is not my life." Even episodes of Oprah (whom I have come to consider my third parent ever since I started watching her in college) seemed to warn me to leave and then affirmed my decision to walk away from it all.

One episode in particular validated my choice. Oprah's guest was Tom Shadyac, who is best known as a movie director for Jim Carrey movies like *Ace Ventura: Pet Detective*. Tom was on the show to talk about his documentary *I Am*, and he explained what led to making the documentary: He had achieved the pinnacle of success in Hollywood, had money and homes everywhere, was jetting around the world in private planes, and had tons of adoration, but ultimately he felt no happier than he was before these accomplishments.

Tom had done everything "right," but in the end, it felt so wrong. He came to ultimately ask the question, "What's wrong with the world and what can we do about it?" Through his documentary, he set out to answer those questions and share the wisdom he gained.

Even though I had achieved nowhere near Tom's level of success, I related to him. I related to the feeling of having everything in the world that you'd think would make you happy and knowing that it didn't. I too felt like something was very wrong with the way our society is driven toward "success," but couldn't articulate what it was. Tom and his film gave me a gift, the understanding that yes, being rich did not mean I must be fulfilled by the money alone.

Deep down, I knew a path of strict financial success would lead me straight to an empty and meaningless existence, as I had seen it do for many rich people around me.

In early 2010, I gave my notice, and had no idea what I'd do next. A friend who also worked in his dad's worker's compensation firm offered me a job, and I took it on a freelance basis. I decided I'd support myself by taking depositions while I figured out what I wanted to do with my life.

It turned out to be a great arrangement and a fantastic new business. Word got around and soon enough I was doing depositions on behalf of a handful of workers compensation attorneys. I worked part-time and made even more than I earned at my dad's firm working full time, and traveled, traveled, traveled. One year, I went to Turks and Caicos three times!

I joined a travel club and discovered an amazing opportunity to travel with an organization that built schools out of trash-stuffed discarded soda bottles in Guatemala. Over just three years, I went to work in Guatemala six times.

Meanwhile, my mom was settling into her retirement from the law firm. She decided to start a non-profit organization so she could help people experience financial stability and security by becoming skilled in dealing with their money, and named it the Financially Fit Foundation.

My mom knew that many people, even those who look successful, struggle with money, feeling like they never have enough. She could show them that their financial state was not a reflection of how generous their boss was toward them or how the economy was doing, but of their financial habits and their relationship to money.

About a year into her venture, she realized how much she preferred a behind-the-scenes role, and she recruited me to lead the workshops for the ever-growing crowd that met in her living room.

We created the curriculum together and I began to lead the workshops—and I loved it. Teaching was totally my thing—*this* offered the kind of difference I wanted to make in people's lives, and it turns out that I'm pretty good at taking dry, complex concepts and making them understandable and entertaining. I'm proud to be effective at helping people to become confident with money, and then show them the tangible steps to take that make it happen.

Our curriculum doesn't tell people how to spend their money. We help each person clearly understand their own values and goals and become aware of how aligned their spending has been (or not!) with those priorities. Then I show them a system that allows them to get their spending, savings, and investments on track with what truly matters to them.

Working with so many people has led me to a profound observation: Most people believe they're unhappy with money because they don't have enough. *They're mistaken!* What really makes them unhappy is that they spend inconsistently with who they think they are or what they want to stand for. In other words, they spend inconsistently with their values.

Of course, people need to cover the necessities, even ones they don't really like, but there is a method to spend and save in a way that honors who you are and what you value. This makes your money a tool for your happiness rather than a weapon of suffering.

In my own life, I am most satisfied when I spend time and money on items and experiences that reflect my values. In part, my obsession with money is a commitment to my values and a desire to live in accordance with them. I am by no means perfect or entirely consistent, but for the most part, I notice how much peace and ease I experience when I'm living according to my values. Aside from teaching, this provides me the most meaning and fulfillment.

Values have become the center of my work.

Let's be clear: I'm not talking surface values such as "I value fast cars and fine wine." That's just ego. I'm talking about deep values based within your character, integrity, and self-knowledge. Learn what makes you, personally, content and fulfilled.

The lack of values (or lack of clarity of our values) is what makes most of us miserable over money and drives us to spend more, more, and more, hoping to find fulfillment.

Living a life that honors your values is the key to your happiness. Now is the time to determine what those values are. Waiting until you become rich will, by my experience, make it less likely that you figure out what they are (unless you go through a personal or professional tragedy that breaks you).

It seems as though having lots of money and "stuff" can be a big distraction, and you'll find it even harder to look within yourself. Not to mention the "yes" people who let you believe what you say and do is acceptable and even brilliant, just so they can enjoy the perks of being in the rich person's orbit.

Let me add this: *Values cannot be bought. They do not arrive through a bank deposit. They are found through your investment into personal study, reflection, and discovery.* Of course, your values may evolve over time; what is important is to remain conscious of what they are throughout your life.

Keep clear about your own worth as a person so you don't slide into the trap of deriving your worth from money. Without your values to keep you anchored, you'll start to feel superior to those with less—and inferior to those with more. While you may feel different, you're not any better or worse than you were before you had money. Oprah says that money just makes you more of who you already are (and of course she's right!).

Any success story, including a rags-to-riches journey, is not complete until your prosperity is matched by your inner wealth, and you feel fulfilled, whole, and content. (You'll know you've succeeded when you're kind and honest with yourself and others.) The road to your inner wealth is paved with values, not diamonds.

There have been many excellent studies into what makes people happy and live long, fulfilled lives. The experts agree on *connection, contribution, purpose,* and *physical activity.* Of course, they mean different things to different people (yoga is a bit different from a triathlon). How do *you* interpret these four keys to happiness and a long life? What are the ways *you* want to experience them? How do *your* values express them?

Figure this out—it's worth a great deal of effort on your part to get it right—then make sure you spend more of your time and money on what you identify as your values than on what matter less to your wellness and happiness.

Remember this about your values: Look for them in what you buy, offer them in what you sell, and embody them— *live* them—as *what you are.* This is what trips most people up: it's only possible to do so if you are firmly grounded in the recognition of your own value and worthiness.

If there's only one thing you take away from me, it's this: I implore you to invest your time and your money into overcoming any negative self-worth issues you may still have. Most of us, including me, need to do this inner work.

Don't be afraid to ask for help, including therapy; don't worry that feeling good about yourself will kill your drive for accomplishment. It doesn't work like that.

I promise you—being happy is the best incentive for success you can have.

Biography

Chelsea is a financial coach and business consultant to millennial entrepreneurs, helping them create financially strong companies with values-based budgets, systems, and cultures. As director of education at the Financially Fit Foundation, she leads personal finance workshops for teenagers and adults. She is also a commercial real estate investor and shows others how to invest.

A progressive commentator and regular panelist on the weekly political podcast The Trump Report on AfterbuzzTV, Chelsea spends much of her airtime arguing that our fundamental problem is the role of money in politics.

Lawyering is her side hustle.

Chelsea graduated from the University of California, Irvine with a B.A. in Social Ecology, received her J.D. from Southwestern Law School in Los Angeles, and has learned enough from Oprah to have earned a Ph.D. Chelsea can't wait for the day that she finally meets her.

Contact Information:

www.chelseagalicia.com
www.financiallyfitfoundation.org
Instagram @chelsea_galicia
Twitter @chelseagalicia

CHAPTER FOUR

The TIKI Factor

Tiki Davis

A screwdriver in my neck at the age of nine nearly ended my life.

As it turned out, that blade would cut away my old existence and slice a path for a new beginning.

A man entered my bedroom and woke me. He asked harshly, *"Where is your mama, kid? Where is your mama, you little bastard? She stole my money!"*

I was not very afraid. I was accustomed to seeing men coming and going all the time in our home, so I sat up on the edge of the bed. "I don't know. Guess she's in the flats." The flats were the housing projects of Odessa, Texas.

But I never saw *this* coming.

The man wrapped a bandana around my neck and tried to strangle me. Then he pushed me back on the bed, jammed a pillow over my head, and started punching me. When I felt the blade of his screwdriver stab through the pillow and into my neck, I twisted away, rolled to the wall, slid down between the wall and the mattress, and dove under the bed.

The man couldn't reach me under the bed, and I curled myself into as small a ball as I could manage. I didn't know I was in danger of bleeding to death, I was just trying to avoid being stabbed or hit again.

He swore, jabbed at me under the bed, yelled at me, but he couldn't reach me. Finally, he gave up. I heard him run away and heard the backdoor slam shut. I waited, feeling the blood running down my T-shirt. After what seemed a long time, I crawled out from under the bed..

I went down the stairs, and as I passed my mama's hatchet, her defense weapon, I felt relief that the man hadn't seen it to use on me.

I staggered next door where my brother Kevin was playing Atari video games with the neighbor kids. I pounded on the door, a woman answered, saw me covered in blood, and screamed. I fell into my brother's arms as he sat on the couch, and he started screaming too, setting off a roomful of hysteria.

The ambulance was called, and I was rushed to the emergency room. Most of my family lived in those projects and word quickly spread to my mother, who was hanging out elsewhere in the flats. Mama arrived at the hospital shortly after the ambulance did.

"Don't say nothin' about what happened!" she warned me.

My mama had stolen money from that man, and because of my unconditional love for her, I never said a word. I understood what my mama did, how she needed to support her drug habit, and I knew how she also supported my brother, me, her sisters, boyfriends, and numerous friends to the best of her ability.

I understood.

I kept my mouth shut.

As I lay on the stretcher, I heard the paramedic tell the doctor, "This kid nearly bled to death. We got him here just in time!"

My stabbing started a roller-coaster of events over the next thirty-plus years, and they're still going on now. The nine-year-old boy is now a 40-year-old man who has weathered peaks and valleys, from a high of being a high school football star in a state where football is king, down to time in a solitary jail cell.

Despite the challenges and obstacles, I would, through God's grace and my persistence, be able to experience events that dreams are made of.

The past has nothing new to say, so I have learned to not listen to it. Yet, I shall never forget the uneven journey through the years, and lessons learned from this ongoing odyssey. My story, which has led to financial success, exoneration in the criminal justice system, and a new career in motivational speaking with creation of the TIKI Factor, continues.

I was born Wednesday, July 27, 1978 in Andrews, Texas. "Wednesday's child is full of woe" seems to be an accurate folk saying, for I would have my share of sorrow and pain mixed with joy and happiness. I was born prematurely, weighing just two pounds, and was so small that I slept in a dresser drawer when my parents brought me home from the hospital. My father, Frank Coulter, and my mother, Karen "Louise" Young, parted company shortly after I was born. Mama named me Tiki after a hotel and gave me her maiden name, Davis, as my surname. My middle name is Frank, apparently as acknowledgement of my parents' relationship.

Mama left me with my father, who also wasn't ready to take care of me. His mother, Grandma Hattie raised me until I was about four. Those few early years were the happiest and safest of my young life, and I wish I could remember more from that time. When Mama came and got me, I lived off and on with her and with her mother. Mama and I stayed in a variety of temporary places, often in motels or with other family members.

While being stabbed was scary and almost fatal, it was just

one of many traumas that happened while I was an on-again, off-again part of my mama's messy life. I became a petty thief, and as the song goes, when I fought against the law, the law usually won.

My education was a patchwork of dozens of different schools, where I struggled until I found a salvation of sorts when I was placed in foster care.

In foster care, I learned for the first time in my life there were actual rewards for doing the right thing. Good behavior, prompt attention to chores, cleanliness, and completing homework assignments earned weekly allowances and often weekend trips to amusement parks, movie theaters, and other fun outings. I even learned some salesmanship skills selling candy door-to-door, and that success in dealing with the public would pay huge dividends decades later.

I was introduced to Pop Warner football and through my God-given strength, speed, and agility, discovered my ability as a running back. Coaches noticed, too, and by the end of my junior season at Odessa High School, I seemed poised for greatness, ready for a standout senior season and already carrying numerous letters of inquiry from major college programs regarding where I might wish to run for a fully-paid college education and possibly a National Football League future.

During my last few years of high school, I finally had some stability with a wonderful foster family, Sam and Joyce Watts and their children, who treated me as one of their own. I had a sweet girlfriend, my own car, and to borrow another song's lyrics, my future was so bright I had to wear shades.

Those shades proved to be blinders, and an encounter derailed my senior football season and all those dreams and hopes. Although I was innocent of the assault charges leveled against me, more than 20 years would pass before my name was cleared. I spent six months in the Ector County Jail, missing my senior year in high school, and by the time I was released, my future seemed as empty as my pockets.

My mother was in prison for murder when I got out of jail, and we managed to have some time together at the prison for a long visit. It was the last time I saw her.

God works in mysterious ways, and at His chosen pace. Thank God He also placed a host of wonderful people in my life, including my foster parents, who remain an integral part of my family. After I received my high school diploma, I went to work at porter and car washer at Bronco Chevrolet in Odessa. I eventually worked myself into position to be a salesman on Saturdays.

Over time, I was noticed by the owner, Steve Late, who took a personal interest in my life. Eventually he said, "Tiki, if you pursue your dream, I will pay your tuition to any college in Texas. As long as you stay in school and make passing grades, tuition will be covered."

I enrolled at Sul Ross State University, about a two-hour drive away, and I did my best to make up for my senior year in high school. I'd strongly felt my year of football glory had been stolen from me, so I tried out for the football team. Though my teenage hopes of stardom were not realized, I was a running back with some playing time and I was thrilled to score a few touchdowns.

When a coaching change meant a change in my playing situation and I was benched, I quit the team. Still making up for my lost senior year, I decided to campaign for Homecoming King and won in a very close election. When I told a university staff member I had achieved my goals and was ready to move on, he stopped me cold with his response: "Yes, Tiki, but have you earned a degree?"

I considered my options, and I am convinced the voice of God reminded me that it was time to grow up; this wasn't meant to be a substitute for high school. It was time to think of my future.

I committed to school and dived into my studies. I also became involved in the university's theatre program and was active in the Black Student Association, Although I no longer was a student-athlete, I convinced several Odessa athletes to enroll at Sul Ross. I earned my bachelor's degree in 2003. I still was on probation for the assault charge and decided to stay in Alpine to work toward a master's degree as well. I completed the requirements two years later.

I had a real breakthrough about this time. I had given up my dream of being a professional athlete at age 22 so that I could focus on my education. I did not want to be a player on the field—I wanted to be a player in life. I made a total commitment to live from my imagination and not my history. They gave me a football and told me to run, but I took the time to educate myself.

Make no mistake, when you make great changes in your life, it will cost you your old life.

Outside the classroom and the stage, my life's journey continued to have highs and lows. My mother died in prison before my final semester of my undergraduate studies, and we sadly buried her on the day of her scheduled release from incarceration.

Shortly after graduation, I launched my movie career, first as an extra, then with a speaking role in *Friday Night Lights*, based on Buzz Bissinger's book about a season of Odessa Permian

High School football, and starring Billy Bob Thornton. The experience and friendships I established would position me for future encounters of the previously-unimaginable kind.

I made another screen appearance in *The Three Burials of Melquiades Estrada,* directed by and starring Tommy Lee Jones, but post-graduation life mainly involved oilfield employment boom and bust—lucrative pay and bonuses followed by layoffs. By then I was married with an infant daughter, and once again, I learned the Lord will not lead you where He will not keep you.

When my daughter was born, I searched for my dad, whom I'd not seen often in my life, and not at all since I was a young boy. I found him in a nearby state, built a relationship with him, and he's a part of my life and my daughter's now.

My long-time habits of keeping some get-away money handy enabled me to buy vehicles and equipment for a mobile car wash, and within months, my earlier car sales experience produced monthly income that approached what I earned in the oilfields. I parlayed my oilfield engineering skills into a successful consulting business, and soon my enterprises expanded into trucking, real estate, residential construction and two successful barbeque restaurants.

My entrepreneurial success earned me several prestigious business awards in the Odessa-Midland area, and I was a millionaire before my thirty-fifth birthday.

Despite numerous appeals to the court system to restore my good name, that cloud lingered over my head. I had achieved the financial success portion of the American dream, yet I felt something was still missing in my life. As Shakespeare wrote, "Who steals my purse steals trash . . . But he that filches from me my good name robs me of that which not enriches him, and makes me poor indeed" (Othello, Act 3, scene 3).

Through my church membership, I became a mentor to teenaged boys and young men, attempting to show them through my own experiences the possibilities available through making positive choices, but my life's work remained unfulfilled.

God once again took my hand and led me to Bishop T.D. Jakes' church, The Potter's House, a large nondenominational church in Dallas, Texas. When Bishop Jakes posed the question, "Are you chosen?" I believed that God spoke to me through his words.

I had been financially rich, yet spiritually broke. It was not until that moment that I knew what was missing: God. There are no paths to success that do not involve God.

Within the next two years, amazing things transpired. My 1996 accuser contacted my attorney and me, recanted the accusation, and through a court order, my name was cleared. I met motivational speaker Les Brown, who heard my story and became my mentor. I continue to travel as a motivational speaker, discussing **The TIKI Factor:**

T=*Total Commitment.*

I=*Imagination.*

K=*Kindred Spirits*, maintaining relationships with positive people with like-minded goals, ethics, and morals

I=*Invest in Yourself.* My story has attracted attention from both the motion picture industry and publishing world.

God has never left my side, guiding me from the depths of poverty to achievements and associations I would never imagined. God makes no mistakes and He directed me on a path that included hardship and heartache because He knew I could overcome. My story is not mine; it belongs to the world to share with others the possibilities available by grace through faith.

Biography

Motivational speaker Tiki Davis' journey of travail to triumph from the
streets to the stage illustrates the determination of man coupled with God's
grace through faith.

He attended Sul Ross State University in Alpine, Texas, earning a
bachelor's degrees in communications, with a minor in theater, and a
master's in liberal arts.

Using engineering experience gained in the West Texas
oilfields, he started his own successful consulting business,
and has interests in real estate, residential construction, and
two successful barbeque restaurants. He was named Odessa's
Black Entrepreneur of the Year and was also honored by the
Odessa Chamber of Commerce. He became a mentor to boys
and young men, telling of his trek through adversity and
stressing the potential benefits of positive choices and good
judgment

Tiki Davis shares his story and *The TIKI Factor* with
churches, corporations, high school, and collegiate athletics
teams, youth groups and organizations, and individuals
committed to making a difference in their own lives and
those of others.

Tiki still lives in the Midland-Odessa area, and he has one
daughter, Brooklynn, 10.

Contact Information:

www.tikidavis.com

Facebook: @thetikifactor
Twitter: @thetikifactor
Instagram: @thetikifactor
You Tube: @thetikifactor

CHAPTER FIVE

There is No 'Secret' to Success

Marie Cosgrove

I magine that at this moment you have everything of which you ever have dreamed. You have the perfect job. You have a perfect family. You have perfect health. You have _____ (fill in the blank). You are a success. Imagine your perfect life.

How would that perfect life be different than your current situation?

If you have all you've ever dreamed about, I suppose you *are* happy and fulfilled. And that's great news. Congratulations to you!

If you are not fulfilled and successful, what are you willing to sacrifice to get what you want? Would you be interested in knowing the secret to obtaining your every dream and desire as well as achieve massive success?

I am sorry to break it to you, but *there is no secret to success.* Despite all the webinars, books, and seminars promising to give you the "secret" to achieving success, you will not find it in some hidden message. You will not find it in a secret potion. You will not find it via a psychic guru, intellectual guru, or once-in-a-lifetime seminar.

However, if you keep reading, you will find one of the formulas for success.

One of my good friends, who recently performed his sold-out comedy act in the Selena Auditorium in Corpus Christi, Texas, laughed when he saw the headline about his act in the local paper: "Overnight Success."

The reality is that it took him years of discipline, determination, and dedication. Yes, that was his formula for success—**discipline, determination, and dedication.**

If you dedicate yourself to these three points, it is possible for you to reach massive success—even millionaire status. Let's review them in some more detail:

Discipline: Are you disciplined enough to do what it takes during your downtime to help you reach success?

For example, when I was a single mom of four young children, I took steps that would help me grow. When I say single parent—I mean it literally. The children's father lost parental rights. I had no child-support. No financial backing. No days off without the kids. Although being a single parent rarely gives you extra time, the downtime I did have I used to study and grow to advance my career. Eventually, I became very successful within the company for which I was working.

Determination: How determined are you to reach success?

Unfortunately, I was fired from the company in which I had achieved great success. Regardless, I maintained my determination to be a success. *Instead of becoming bitter, I decided to become better.* I had to reinvent myself and stay determined. I started a new career with another company and eventually earned enough to start my own company.

Dedication: Olympic Gold Medalist Jesse Owens said, "We all have dreams. But to make dreams into reality, it takes an awful lot of determination, dedication, self-discipline, and effort."

Imagine my shock at being fired after I had given up so much to reach a high level of success. I was the top national sales representative for the company that fired me. My dedication did not diminish when I was fired. In fact, instead of being diminished, my dedication grew stronger. Within two years and with much hard work, discipline, determination, and dedication, I bought the company that had fired me.

When I purchased the company, many in my industry predicted I would bankrupt it and myself within six months. Eight years later, we are still strong—proving that the three success principles—discipline, determination, and dedication—are the ones you cannot afford to ignore if you want to reach success.

Never Stop Learning

I am incredibly blessed to have been raised by my grandparents. My grandfather taught me important lessons that helped me reach success and that I continue to follow today: *Never stop learning. Always have a teachable spirit! You need to exercise your mind just as much as you exercise your body.*

He went on to explain, "The more you exercise, the stronger your muscles become. It is the same way with the brain; you need to feed it, use it, and keep it engaged. Always keep learning and using your brain because it is a muscle. Learning is something you just keep doing, whether you are a baby, or 100 years old, you will never 'know it all.'"

I recall the day my grandfather retired and sold his barbershop. The very same day he retired, he enrolled at the local college to keep his mind active and engaged for the same reason he walked to work every day—to keep fit.

My grandfather's barbershop is also the place where I developed my love of reading and learning. I would spend afternoons reading his comic-book collection and *National Geographic*. He gave a free comic book to every child who got a haircut. I always made sure I had read my grandfather's new comics before he gave them away.

National Geographic gave me an opportunity to "travel" the world. When I was a child in Texas, we did not travel outside of own large state. *National Geographic* gave me a glimpse into an entirely different world and an opportunity to learn about different animals, nature, and cultures.

I was reminded of my grandfather's words when I read a story about a time when one of the greatest artists of all time, Michelangelo, was asked to provide a talk on art at the age of 87. His reply was, "ancora imparo," which means "I'm still learning." Michelangelo had a teachable spirit and true humility.

As a 48-year-old woman with four adult children, three grandchildren, and a little one still at home, I continue on the path of life-long learning that my grandpa showed me. Along the way, I have learned some valuable lessons that have helped me continue.

Humility—Maintain a teachable spirit. Remaining humble is necessary to develop a sincere heart and a desire for learning.

Responsibility—Take the first step in learning. Being prepared to act when presented with new learning opportunities is assuming responsibility for your own growth and success.

Defeat—The greatest motivator for learning. I love the example of Benjamin Franklin; he was brilliant and loved learning, but his parents could not afford to keep him in school. He had to leave and go to work when he was only ten years old, but despite this setback, he persevered. He became an inventor, an author, and perhaps the most famous founding father of our beautiful nation.

Difficulties—Opportunities for learning. Looking back at my life, one of the greatest challenges I faced was being fired when I was the sole financial supporter of my household with four small children at home. My dire situation forced me to learn new skill sets and opportunities in a different field.

Maturity—Learning values. A mature person recognizes the need to seek wisdom and appreciates learning opportunities. In contrast, an immature person believes she is intellectually superior and places little value on continued education that may lead to advancement, growth, and success, essentially capping their full potential.

The Break Through gives you numerous examples of people who struggled through challenges and used the above five lessons in learning to succeed when they faced difficulties, loss, or defeat.

As you examine where you are in the five levels of learning, why not adopt *ancora imparo* as your motto? Dedicate yourself to accept and nurture learning opportunities that may come your way. Embrace the difficulties and defeats that will catapult you to new learning breakthroughs.

Legacy

What do you want your own legacy to be? Do the actions you take today leave a legacy to be carried in people's hearts for generations to come?

I vividly remember enjoying one glorious, warm autumn afternoon, highly unusual weather for Dayton, Ohio. I was in the car with my family and overwhelmingly happy.

Then the phone rang. My brother-in-law gave us horrible news. I went from overwhelmingly happy to overwhelmingly sad—emotionally going from zero to sixty as I heard my brother-in-law say, "Dad was diagnosed with pancreatic cancer."

The tears would not stop flowing. My heart hurt so deeply. My heart hurt for the entire family. I have been in the medical field for over 15 years—from what I know, pancreatic cancer has one of the highest mortality rates.

My youngest son was seven years old at the time. I could not picture him growing up without his grandfather—the only one he had left.

I have loving memories of my grandfather who helped raise me. I was fortunate enough to spend time with him throughout my entire childhood, and I learned my most valuable lessons from him, such as "never stop learning." I cannot imagine what life would have been without my grandfather; he made my childhood unforgettable.

I wanted my son to build lasting memories through his relationship with his grandfather, like those I was blessed to have with my grandfather.

We went to South Dakota the first opportunity we had to spend some quality time with my father-in-law.

I began to ask my father-in-law questions to learn more about him. I will never forget the answer to the question, "What is the one thing that you wish everyone knew?"

He said, "*Everyone* has an expiration date. Some of us know the date, but most of us do not. How you live your life *before* your expiration date is what matters."

He shared a story about an inmate who was on death-row and had accepted Christ. On the day he was to be executed, he had a huge smile. The other inmates asked him, "Why are you smiling? Don't you realize you will be executed today?"

The inmate replied, "All of us have an expiration date—except most of us don't know the date, but I do know mine! I am happy because today I meet my maker and savior!"

My father-in-law was also a man of faith. He had dedicated his life to serving others. He voluntarily gave his time freely to underprivileged, at-risk youth so that they can grow emotionally, mentally, and spiritually to hopefully break free from things that held them back.

Dolly Parton said, "If your actions create a legacy that inspires others to dream more, learn more, do more, and become more, then, you are an excellent leader."

My father-in-law also devoted his time to serving his family through his life's example and by giving them words of wisdom so they could be spiritually filled, leaving behind a legacy that lives on in the hearts of those he loved and onto a thousand generations.

There are some questions you can ask yourself to help you build a legacy you can be proud of for years to come. A legacy that will not only survive materially but also will survive in the hearts and minds of those you love after your 'expiration' date—an expiration date we will all experience.

What are the contents of your book?

My father-in-law taught me through the way he lived his life that *your life is your book*. What does your life look like in the chapters you have written?

What actions are you taking today that will impact the way people remember you? Will the actions you take today leave a legacy to be carried in people's hearts for generations to come?

I will always be thankful for the small gestures my father-in-law has shown me; they have left a significant impact on my heart. When I was pregnant with my son, he called me frequently to make sure my pregnancy was coming along well. He encouraged me when I was feeling 'blue.' He had an ear for listening. He took time away from running the farm to call his daughter-in-law, which showed me that he genuinely cared and valued me as a person. His actions showed me he had a kind, loving spirit.

What do you want your legacy to be?

You can make changes in the way you live your life today so you can leave behind a powerful, impactful legacy. You can determine *now* how others will remember you. Your legacy can be the most extraordinary, unforgettable, and valuable inheritance for those you love.

Biography

Marie Cosgrove is a successful entre-
preneur with a proven track record of
turning failing companies into profit
centers. Among her successes is being
fired from a medical device manu-
facturer specializing in developing
devices to help doctors diagnose con-
cussions, traumatic brain injuries,
dizziness, and vertigo, to purchasing
this same company who had fired her. Eight years later, she
continues to lead this company and has taken it international.
She also grew a start-up medical device company specializing
in arterial and vascular diagnostic solutions into a 14-million-
dollar company within two years.

Marie has over 15 years' experience in the medical industry
where she closely works with top neurologists and medical
researchers on the brain's ability to rebuild neuropathways,
which until recently was thought to be impossible. A renowned
international speaker, she talks about how we can rebuild these
neurological connections, strengthen cognitive ability, and
"unleash the genius mind" that is inside us all.

She has shared the stage with motivational speaker Les
Brown and *New York Times* best-selling authors Brian Tracy and
John Maxwell. Marie serves on the Forbes Coaches Council
and as President of the Advisory Council for the John Maxwell
Team. She has been featured in *Hispanic Executive* magazine
and recently won the I Change Nations Golden Rule Award.

Marie is a Certified Facilitator Instructor in the Round Table Method, by Global Priority Solutions, Certified Human Behavioral Coach, Dr. Paul Scheele Learning Systems, 'Reclaim the Brilliance" Certified Trainer, Certified DISC Personality Profile Facilitator, Business Coach, and Trainer.

She is the founder of The Virtue Project, a nonprofit specialized in assisting single moms and troubled teens learn personal, professional, and entrepreneurial skills for success.

Contact Information:

You can follow Marie at:
www.mariecosgrove.com
Facebook: https://www.facebook.com/marie.l.cosgrove
LinkedIn: www.linkedin.com/in/balanceback
Instagram: https://www.instagram.com/marie.cosgrove/
www.thevirtueproject.org

CHAPTER SIX

Break Through with HOPE³

Helping Other People Excel, Evolve, and Enjoy

Dr. Caryn Darwin

L ife is a complicated thousand-piece puzzle—when you believe you have found the piece that perfectly aligns to complete the picture, it usually does not quite fit. When you find the *right* piece, everything fits into place and the scattered pieces all work together to become a masterfully designed mosaic.

This has been my life. Much of what has happened made absolutely no sense at the time, yet in the grand scheme of things, every piece of my past is a critical piece of who I am now.

I am a licensed specialist in school psychology and a licensed psychologist. I had no intention of studying psychology. In fact, as an undergraduate, I started as a business major with plans to make big money.

Still, human behavior always fascinated me and I was interested in what motivated people. Whenever I am asked why I chose the mental health field, I say with a straight face, "My family was my inspiration because we put the funk in dysfunctional."

I grew up in Chattanooga, Tennessee. My father worked for the Chattanooga Public Works, and my mother was a nursing assistant. My father was barely literate and left school after sixth grade, and my mother was a high school dropout.

When I was young, my older sisters moved out and it was just my younger brother and me at home with my parents. They loved us and provided for me and my siblings, but their drinking and "crazy love" version of domestic violence were rough on us all.

High-decibel arguments punctuated by punching, stabbing with pocket knives and butcher knives, kicking, and screaming were commonplace in our home on the weekends. A gun was involved just once, thank God.

The pattern was always the same. Mom and Dad went to their favorite liquor store on Friday night and grabbed a bottle of whiskey. The evenings started peacefully; my parents relaxed, played records (and boy, did they have a record collection!), laughed, and joked around.

After hours of drinking, my mom began to pick fights with my dad, accusing him of infidelity or listing his shortcomings as a man. He would react. Soon they would reach a point of no return and the battles would begin. The night typically ended with my mom passed out on the floor with a black eye, a busted lip, and God knows what else, and Dad would have bolted. For added drama, we might have a visit from the police.

My parents divorced when I was in second grade. Before I had a chance to process it, Mama introduced us to our new stepfather.

At first, things were quiet. Our stepfather either hung out in his old neighborhood, smoked joints at our house, or he was gone in the streets. Things soon took a turn for the worse and they fought, but my stepfather usually left the house instead of arguing with mom. After a couple of drinks one night, Mom decided to track him down and confront him. She did not have a babysitter, so she took us kids along in her yellow Thunderbird. She loved that car!

Mom found her husband in a bar and they argued while we kids waited in the car. Their fight spiraled out of control and the police showed up. When my mother refused to calm down, she was handcuffed and put in the back of a patrol car, charged with driving under the influence of alcohol, resisting arrest, and perhaps even child endangerment.

My brother and I watched as the police drove her away to jail. A friendly officer explained he was taking us to a safe place, and they would reach out to our family to see if anyone could pick us up. We learned we would go to foster care if we were not picked up from the shelter in 30 days.

My brother was only four so he was put with the infants and toddlers and I was with the children and adolescents. It was frightening to be separated and away from family, but I did my best to cooperate.

What I learned at the shelter changed the way I saw the world. I learned advocacy skills, and that planted a seed inside of me that continues to grow as I work with students to help them overcome their obstacles. I also realized other people observed *my* behavior, and the people there actually cared for our welfare.

I lived up to my last name—Darwin—and learned to adapt and evolve. In the back of my mind I worried about foster care and the 30-day deadline.

After three weeks, my father showed up to rescue us. We spent a few stressful days with him and his new wife before he sent us to live with an aunt.

That year I was eight years old. Watching *The Cosby Show* changed the direction of my life when I decided to become a doctor like Dr. Huxtable.

I *totally* comprehend *The Cosby Show* was fictional, but it depicted the ideal of American life, let alone African-American life! Was it possible for black people in America to live this way? The Cosbys never ate pig's ears, pig's feet, sugar water, or mayonnaise sandwiches like we did when funds were low, and when there was family conflict, it was always resolved before 8:30 p.m. (with no fist fights or blood).

I wanted that for myself.

When my mom's year-long sentence was up, she and my father showed up together at my aunt's home. I was shocked. What happened to my father's new wife? How could my parents get back together? Could I trust them? (If I could not trust my parents, then who in the world could I trust?)

I learned my parents were in the process of reconciliation. In the meantime, my mother moved us into a couple of dangerous living situations while she attempted to get her life back on track.

Even with the stressful moves, I enjoyed school. I participated in a research project for the first time, a technical one on the HIV and AIDS epidemic. I was even tested for a gifted program, and the realization that I was smart started to sink in.

When I look back, it blows my mind that I began my journey to excellence during one of the most tumultuous and unstable times in my life.

As another school year concluded, my parents officially

reunited. Things were blessedly calmer for a while, then the drinking and fighting started again.

One day after a brawl, my mother slipped on the kitchen floor and broke her leg; she was in a cast for what seemed like an eternity. Soon after this incident, my parents' lives finally turned around. We bought a house, where I lived the remainder of my childhood, and my parents began attending church. After they rededicated their lives to Christ, the domestic violence slowed down, but it never truly stopped until my father died.

I love my parents, yet I do not hesitate to share their story. Their lives are proof that unresolved hurt and baggage from the past leads to self-destruction.

As I transitioned to middle school, I became more comfortable with being intelligent and nerdy. What I most loved about being a nerd is that no matter what went on in my life, I could always control how much I excelled.

In 1993, my father suddenly became extremely ill, and his diagnosis was shocking—he had HIV. As I sobbed inconsolably, a small voice in the back of my head asked, "But what about Mama? Is she HIV positive too?" She would not tell me.

Years earlier, I had participated in that HIV/AIDs project, and I knew what was happening as my father disintegrated. My mother was amazing, and she utilized her nursing skills and cared for my father until the very end.

I continued my nerdiness in high school, graduated in the top 10 of my class, and was blessed enough to receive scholarships to cover my entire college tuition and living expenses at two state schools. I decided to attend Austin Peay State University in Clarksville, Tennessee.

Tragedy struck again the spring of my freshman year. As I was riding home with a classmate, a vehicle attempted to run my friend's vehicle off the road. Her car spun out of control and we hit a guard rail. My brief life flashed before my eyes and I thought I had died.

My injuries included a broken femur, fractured pelvis, collapsed lungs, and post-traumatic mental scars. The bill was more than $100,000 for two days in the hospital.

I did not have medical insurance, and I was terrified that everything I had would be taken away in the blink of an eye. Thank God, a hospital social worker arranged for insurance that would cover most of my medical expenses, because I was in the hospital for a month. Lying in my hospital bed, I was unsure of my fate and my future. Would I walk again? Would I have some sort of permanent disability? Could I go back to college?

I laid on my backside at home for two more months as my mother took a leave of absence and used her nursing skills again. She was such a loving and caring spirit! I am sure she was terrified about how we would survive, but she never complained.

When it was time to walk, I fell down every time I stood up because my muscles had atrophied. But guess what? I got back up again and again because I was determined to walk and recover—I refused to lose!

After weeks of intensive physical therapy, I rose up and I did *not* fall. That fall semester, I returned to college, which was a miracle.

You know, I believe people must almost die before they give themselves permission to live! I have received this reminder several times over my short life and I heeded the message.

I switched my major to psychology and figured I might as well determine if I wanted to work with troubled youth—ones just like me (it seemed I always was just one bad decision away from being one myself). While I was in school, I worked at a girls' home for troubled youth and at homes for adults with severe mental disabilities, and it solidified my desire to work with children and young adults with challenges.

I graduated with my degree in psychology in May 2000. Without a pause, I moved on to graduate school to earn a master's degree in psychology and an education specialist certification so I could become a school psychologist in Tennessee.

Because I never forgot my desire to be a doctor, after five years in several Nashville area school systems, I decided it was time to get my doctorate. Come hell or high water, I would be Dr. Caryn Darwin.

There was a small glitch. My mother died immediately before I was to start my doctoral studies the Fall 2009. I was heartbroken and overwhelmed with grief. I loved my kind, hardworking, and funny mother. My suspicions regarding her HIV status were accurate; she died of pneumonia because of AIDS-related complex.

Now school was the last thing on my mind. My mother was gone. Who would encourage me now? Although we had our issues and I did not always trust her judgment, she was all I had. How could I move forward with my life?

I postponed school. My little brother was an issue, too. Mama was all he had in this world and he was grief stricken and confused. I knew I had to help my brother, get him on his feet, teach him to drive and manage money, and learn some autonomy. We both got some professional counseling, as well.

Counseling was the best gift I have ever given to myself! The counselor did not allow me to make excuses, and she gave me excellent strategies to deal with my pain.

I started school for my doctorate in 2010; I knew it would

not be easy because I did not have the luxury of quitting my job and going to school full-time. It took six years of days, nights, and weekends before I finished my doctoral coursework.

There was no time to bask in the awards I earned. Now I had to find, get accepted by, and complete a doctoral internship (which would require me to quit my day job), research and write a dissertation, take some exceptionally tough exams, and get a post-doctoral fellowship so I could become a licensed psychologist.

Step one was the internship. After a lot of disappointment, I had a great phone interview with a juvenile detention center in Rockdale, Texas.

Where in the hell is Rockdale? I was about to find out, because the interview told me this was the place I belonged. I would work with urban children from tough backgrounds who had been adjudicated through the juvenile justice system for all types of crimes including armed robbery, selling drugs, and sex offenses.

There was one slight hiccup—it paid only forty percent of the income I had been making. How in the world could I survive? My bills would not stop!

Always remember, if you have faith, God provides. I knew I needed a miracle—and a miracle is what happened. I applied for a scholarship for doctoral students who had completed All But Dissertation (ABD). To my astonishment, I received a one-year stipend that paid the difference in my living expenses. It was nothing but a miracle.

On July 31, 2014, the five-year anniversary of my mother's death, I moved to Texas and began to learn the Texas way of life where everything is bigger and better. So much so, that one of the major grocery stores is named H-E-B, which is an acronym for Here Everything is Better!

My internship was scary, fun, and unnerving all at once, and it pushed me outside of my comfort zone as a clinician. It was so different from the Nashville area school districts where I had worked before.

As my internship began to wrap up, I became nervous (no, terrified!) about locking down a post-doctoral fellowship, the next step to becoming a licensed psychologist.

Should I return to Tennessee or stay in Texas? After much contemplation and prayer, I decided to stay in Texas. It is a huge state with vast opportunities and I did not want to miss out on any coming my way.

I transferred my school psychologist certification from Tennessee to Texas. Finding employment was not as simple as I thought, but finally I found a position near Houston that seemed perfect, and they called me in for an interview for the full-time paid fellowship program. *Jackpot!* When I left the interview, I floated back to my hotel because I was sure that position was mine.

Meanwhile, I desperately continued to seek out school districts to conduct my dissertation research. When I discovered a school-wide positive behavior support conference in Houston (my dissertation topic), something told me to take a leap of faith and pay the registration fee.

I attended the Houston conference calmly assured I would discover exactly what I needed in God's perfect timing. The final puzzle pieces began to assemble haphazardly. I met a gentleman at the conference who not only was employed by the regional headquarters, but also principal at an alternative learning center where I had just applied for a job!

He connected me with another district where I could complete my research. His district, where I interviewed, offered me a position.

That year, I worked fulltime and collected the data I needed to write my dissertation. The day I typed the last period on the last sentence of my dissertation, I cried tears of joy, but the process *still* was not over.

A meeting to "defend" my dissertation was held in Nashville. It went well, and I submitted the final draft on March 24, 2016.

I graduated as Dr. Caryn Darwin just six weeks later.

The commencement speaker talked most appropriately about moonshots and going far beyond what one could imagine. She reminded us that John F. Kennedy had the literal moonshot dream of putting a man on the moon.

My graduation symbolized completion—a dream's coming of age, one that started 30 years earlier when I was eight years old. It too felt like a moonshot!

All my life I have felt I was one poor decision away from ruining my life, or one great decision away from achieving my wildest dreams. Finally, I knew which path I was taking.

With my brand-new degree in hand, I tackled the national licensing exam required for all U.S. psychologists. For 18 months, I spent my evenings and weekends studying every area of psychology known to man. Behold, on the afternoon of December 27, 2017, I passed the exam. Hallelujah!

So now I ask you: What dreams has God placed in *your* heart that you ignore because you fear failure, rejection, or success?

The key to achieving your dreams is to let go and surrender them to God. He gave you those dreams in the first place, so why would He leave you even one second before you have the opportunity to become your greatest self?

Do not give up on your crazy moonshot dream; instead, experience a breakthrough that can change your life *forever*.

Never lose hope.

Biography

Originally from Chattanooga, Tennessee, Dr. Darwin currently resides in Houston, Texas. She completed her Bachelor's, Master's and Education Specialist degrees at Austin Peay State University in Clarksville, Tennessee, and earned her Ph.D. in School Psychology from Tennessee State University in Nashville.

Dr. Darwin is currently employed as a licensed specialist in school psychology in the Houston area and as a licensed psychologist in a private clinic conducting evaluations primarily with children in foster care.

Dr. Darwin's research and clinical interests include the impact of trauma and ecological factors on social/emotional, behavioral, and academic functioning; advocacy and fostering self-determination in youth; positive behavior intervention supports; restorative justice principles and practices; and dismantling the school-to-prison pipeline.

She has presented at both state and national conferences on disruptive behavior disorders and crisis intervention and has been published in several professional publications.

Her passions include traveling, learning about new cultures, reading, bargain shopping, meeting new people, networking, personal growth and development, health and fitness, and living life on purpose with purpose.

Contact Information:

www.linkedin.com/in/caryn-d-900b6519
https://twitter.com/mscaryn
https://www.instagram.com/dcaryn3/
https://www.facebook.com/caryn.darwin

CHAPTER SEVEN

Never Give Up!

Marco Da Veiga

I am sitting in a coffee shop in Oslo, working on my book, writing to you. Why?

Because I have faith that I can help you, and I believe the Almighty Creator will lend a helping hand.

As I write this, I see I have had a lot of victories and breakthroughs in life. My failures, though, have given me wisdom; wisdom has taught me patience, and patience has given me the gift of hope. Hope has made me greater, better, and stronger.

Whenever we travel to reach one objective in the series of goals we set for ourselves, we can easily visualize that we are traveling from one mountaintop to the next mountaintop.

What's important to understand is this: *Between every set of mountaintops, there is a valley.* The valley is tough; this is where your character is tested and you will be pushed to your absolute limits. You will be forced to bring out the best in yourself so that you can overcome the challenges and reach the next peak.

Yea, though I walk through the valley of the shadow of death, I will fear no evil; for You are with me; Your rod and Your staff, they comfort me. —**Psalms 23:4, New King James Version**

On your journey, you always need to acknowledge God and

His presence. He will help you stay focused and keep a good attitude, because there is no room for distractions in the valleys.

Let's talk about valleys.

One of my valleys was a very deep one. I resigned from a job I loved and in which I excelled to go into business with a woman I had met in church. She spoke confidently about her contract with international brand makers and said she was working on a collaboration with Europe and the United States.

I pulled on my gloves and went to work with her for free. I sold my house, my BMW, and went all in. I uprooted my son Marcus and we moved to where my new partner lived. I promised I would help her for six months on this project and help her restore another company as I worked on a new project of my own in Morocco.

Though I believed in my business partner and what she said, as time went by I realized I'd been deceived. Everything about her was a lie and an illusion. My mistake was being too trusting in her as an individual and not researching her well enough. I realized that what I thought was the truth was not true.

I had made a big mistake.

Even though I was in the valley, this experience reinforced my belief that we should always build good relationships on trust, manners, and honesty. I continued to make good connections with new people as I traveled to Germany, London, and Turkey on this doomed business.

I was in a good place, but with the wrong partner. Finally, I had seen what I am capable of doing—running three companies at the same time, working late, waking up early, and doing what needed to be done while I built relationships. It was time for me to be on my own. After five painful months, I left.

Though I felt I was in the wilderness, I followed up on my

new contacts and relationships. After careful thought, I decided to move ahead with my Turkey-to-Morocco clothing import business.

I can do all things through Christ who strengthens me.— **Philippians 4:13 (NKJV)**

My travel to Turkey increased to two or three times per month and trips to Morocco were even more frequent. I set up my company in Agadir, Morocco, negotiating with the bank director, who became a great friend of mine, and going to the court to set up the structure of the company—and did all of this in French.

I tell you, I had to hold on to the word of God and trust Him like a child holds on to his parents. I cannot explain the trauma, pain, and mental toughness it took to survive and sustain myself.

*Cast your burden on the LORD, And He shall sustain you; He shall never permit the righteous to be moved.—***Psalms 55:22 (NKJV)**

I had invested nearly $40,000 in setting up my new business, after everything was done and told with the costs and traveling. Six weeks before my shop was supposed to open, all was looking well, everything was organized, the logistics and customs were in order. I was on a mountaintop.

Then, disaster. Morocco increased the tariff on clothes coming from Turkey by 50%. All of my profits were gone, lost. I had to pull out before the loss became even greater, and for the next two months, I traveled back and forth between Norway and Morocco to make sure the shutdown and all cancellations of contracts went smoothly and legally.

I suffered a great loss and my mind was just boiling. "I lost it all," I thought. The choices I'd made put me in a tough situation, and I was doing all I could to maintain the right attitude, to believe in myself, and to push forward, but honestly, I was drained. It's as though I'd been poured out like water.

It is good for me that I have been afflicted, That I may learn Your statutes.—**Psalms 119:71 (NKJV)**

I had to make some tough decisions, and I did, and I stand behind them and take full responsibility. I made mistakes, but if you don't take risks and make mistakes, you will not succeed. So, to those who are reading this book, *stand strong and keep marching forward.*

There are beauty and love in the results of my failure and mistake.

This is the beauty: If I had stayed at my job, I would never have sold my house and cars. I would never had been able to travel with my son to Dallas, where he was baptized at the Potter's House, and where I was baptized again.

This is the love: I never would have had the opportunity, chance, or time to travel to Nigeria where I met my best friend, now my beautiful wife, my Princess. (By the way, Princess is her real name.)

My journey of hardship, experience, pain, tears, and the endless travel to England, Turkey, Morocco, and Nigeria, made me reflect. Finally, I understood that it all had a reason and a purpose.

This is why I say: *Never give up.*

I give God all the glory for this great breakthrough, for His faithfulness and loving kindness. I would not have made it without my Lord and Savior Jesus Christ.

Every good gift and every perfect gift is from above, and comes down from the Father of lights, with whom there is no variation or shadow of turning.—**James 1:17 (NKJV)**

Believe in yourself, push toward the goals and dreams you have, *just be prepared*, because life will inevitably mow you down at some point. Keep God close by your side at all times. And while no book or audio can completely prepare you for the blow, a good background in personal development, reading, and sharpening your skills will give you a chance.

I am a living witness. I am living my dream, fulfilling my purpose, but *only because I was threshed and humbled*. I grew by being stretched and pulled into uncomfortable and even unbearable positions—but look at me now! I made it and I broke through.

Recently, I was in Lagos, Nigeria, where I hold workshops on leadership and management for Nigerian youth. The university in Lagos is supporting my charitable organization, and as I write this, we're finalizing our business plan and budget. I will be able to reach and inspire young people in a country with more than 100 million people under the age of 30.

This has been a lifelong dream, and despite all the setbacks and pain, I have never been happier or more fulfilled. In life we learn so much every day. All the experience we gain from it—good or bad—is priceless. Now there are a lot of ways to prepare oneself, to get ready and tackle the challenges and difficulties that may come along your way, and I am going to share my best with you.

The Big Five States of Mind

Use these states of mind to prepare you for your walk through the valley and the wilderness as you journey from mountaintop to mountaintop.

Before you start, understand there is no difficulty greater than your capacity to solve it. Remember, you are never alone.

Faith. *You must have faith;* it makes all things possible. The

Bible tells you that faith can move mountains, that you only need faith the size of a tiny mustard seed, and that everything is possible for he who has faith, for all things are possible for God.

Whether you believe in God or not is not the point—*faith* is the point!

Believe in *yourself*, have faith that you *can* and *will*: Yes, you must reach your goal, you will finish your task, you must make it on time, things will work out for you, and you are going to make it!

Though I can't begin to express how important it is for you to have faith, I ask you to trust me and follow me on this first of the big five daily disciplines—have faith.

I ask you to trust me and I will not lead you astray, for you are my brother and sister. Have faith!

Hope. I love hope, because when things are really difficult, I always hope; I say to myself, *Everything's gonna be all right.* One of the world's greatest musicians ever, Bob Marley, says it beautifully in his song "Three Little Birds" when he tells you to not worry about anything because *every* little thing will be all right.

Yes, hope for the best. When your hope is combined with faith, you'll really know that every little thing *will* work itself out. You still might have to fight and stand firm for what you want, but hope will keep your head above water, always!

Please trust me here, too, and take this sweet mellow vibe called *hope* to your heart. Use it in your life to overcome your challenges, for you are greater than any wall that blocks you!

Love. Love is the greatest state of mind. Love caused the creation of all things—that's why we're here. Love makes the world function!

80

When you carry love in your heart and learn to love yourself in truth and in spirit, you can then love your neighbors. You're a master of humanism and on the path of righteousness.

Sometimes it's hard to love because you're afraid your heart will get hurt, but don't let this stop you. Learn how to protect your heart; use your experience to know when and how you should open your heart to others. In any case, you can still love.

I don't know who you are yet, but I love you. I want the best for you. I support you in all that you do as long as your deeds are good and positive.

If you can love me, and I love you plus all the other seven billion people in the world, then I am asking *you* to *also* love the seven billion others.

Why? Because there is something in them that is similar to the thing you love about me. So find it, be humble, and love and respect each other. At least don't hate or fight, even if you can't get along.

I am asking you to trust me, embrace love, and use it as a guide and force in your life. (Don't forget to teach your children how to love, for charity begins at home.)

Positive. Positivity is a game changer, and I can't emphasize enough how important it is for you to be positive. When you are in a positive mental state of mind, you become unstoppable. Being positive is being on another vibration and on a higher frequency! A righteous man's vibration is always positive.

It took me some time to grasp the full depth and importance of being and staying positive.

I have had a lot of ups and downs and I've encountered challenges as I was moving from one mountaintop to another. By being positive and telling myself with faith, hope and love *#everything is gonna be alright*, I got through whatever it was

I had to go through. In every case, my experience became a life changer.

So smile and be happy even when things are really hard. Dig down deep in your soul and give thanks for whatever you are learning. As I said earlier and I'm happy to repeat, *There are no difficulties greater than your capacity to solve them.*

Decide now that you are going to be a positive person! The effect it's gonna have on your life and those around you will be fantastic, but there's more than that. Positivity is also energy that you as a human being send out to this world and universe.

If negative friends or family members pull you down, drain you, and give you less then you give back to them, don't spend as much time with them.

Either you change your friends, or you *change* your friends!

Wake up and live! Be a positive soul, be part of the positive vibration!

Optimistic: I love to be optimistic; it just makes me feel good to have a mindset that things will always work out, that after rain comes sun and through darkness comes light.

Inhale and embrace this thing we call optimism and use it in your daily actions; carry it in your heart.

I know the first time you read this book, you may stop, contemplate the five states of mind, and say, "Yes, I'll give one or two of them a shot." That's not enough. I ask and beg you to make every one of them a *habit*, because when you become a master of the Big Five, you will really feel alive.

Practice these daily disciplines and make them a part of your lifestyle so that you will be a good human being. These mental habits will give you the strength and courage you need to keep pushing for whatever it is you want in your life! Remember, this is *your* life and you can design it however you want.

It's not always gonna be easy to reach your goal, but it sure is possible. Trust me when I say that the Big Five will help you get there, they will make you get there!

The only way you can lose in anything in life is if you give up! *Never give up!* Be an optimistic person. Say out loud, *I am going to make it!*

Say it again: . . . ***I am going to make it!!!***

Biography

Though Marco's family is from the Cape Verde Islands, he was born and raised in Norway. During his childhood, Marco suffered discrimination and harassment; he credited his survival to his strong belief in God.

As he matured and continued to fight against the forces of hate and intolerance, Marco evolved into the leader, teacher and entrepreneur he was born to be. He's a graduate of University of Oslo, where he studied early childhood and youth work.

Marco began his outreach by founding Youth United after an apprenticeship in African Youth in Norway, OMOD and Antiracist Center. He's ambassador of Youths Against Violence in Oslo.

He is the Norwegian rap champion, beginning his recording career in 2005, when he released his first single and music video. In 2008, the music video "O.D. 98" was showcased on MTV, The Voice TV and other media as part of a CD compilation, *Let Me Be Heard*. He reached the semifinal of *Norway Got Talent in 2011*, with an original song that he wrote to his son. In 2012, Marco played Bob Marley in "The Legends" at the Norwegian Opera & Ballet and Nordic Black Theater.

He has performed and given talks in South Africa, Sweden, Nigeria, Denmark, Trinidad, Senegal, Cape Verde, the United States, England, and Norway on TV, radio, and in many locations.

Currently, Marco is the CEO of both Youth Nation, a charitable organization with a mission to *"Restore faith and hope through leadership and management,"* and a consulting/teaching company, Born to Inspire.

Marco is married to Princess, and he has a son, Marcus. He divides his time between his work in Nigeria and his permanent home in Norway.

Contact Information:

Marco Da Veiga
Mobile: (+47) 40469602
Email: mdvunited@gmail.com
Instagram: @marcodaveiga
Twitter: @marcodaveiga
Facebook: www.facebook.com/marcodaveiga
www.marcodaveiga.com

CHAPTER EIGHT

你 做 得 到
(You Got This)

Stacy Ho

In 2016, I was sitting in a van, heading to the airport. With a breaking voice and tears in my eyes, I said, "You know, I always thought I would be the wife of a Rotary President. I never thought it'd be me as Rotary President."

"Stacy, you've done well," Past President George assured me.

The certainty in his voice went straight to my heart. I never thought I would be the hero of my story. I always imagined playing a supporting role.

My story starts quite unassumingly.

Ten years ago, I lived in a perfect bubble. I was raised in a wholesome loving family of seven. My parents had five children and I was in the exact middle.

At this point of my story, I need to tell you that my mother is an amazing woman who is kind, loving, emotionally supportive, and the greatest mom in the world. I do not mention her a lot here because this story is about my father and what he taught me. I am fortunate and grateful to have had two tremendous parents who shaped me into who I am today.

My father was an entrepreneur. He was magical. He

was a fighter. My father grew up as a tycoon's son. Due to a combination of inopportune business choices and post-war market conditions, my grandfather lost his wealth and never recovered. My father told me that my grandfather was only 50 years old when he lost his wealth. My father did not understand why his dad could not find it within himself to rise again. As a result of experiencing the rise and fall of my grandfather's business empire, I believe my father developed his phoenix personality.

A phoenix is a magnificently feathered mythical creature that dies and rises from the ashes—born again from defeat. My dad always told me he was a phoenix. When we experienced low times in our family business, my dad would put on a smile and a fighting spirit and head out to the world. He had a saying that went, *"Another day, another way! We must keep on going! And never say die!"*

Unfortunately, I speak of my father in the past tense because he left this world in 2011. His death was the hardest period in my life.

I was twenty-four when my dad was given a three-year prognosis. Receiving the news from my parents was so unreal. It was the biggest shock of my life. Words. Words. Words.

Words like:

Multiple Myeloma.

Terminal cancer.

Rare.

Incurable.

No proven treatment.

Three years.

The news hit me hard.

I would be losing my loving father, best friend, mentor,

boss, soundboard, and so much more. I also would be losing all my imagined/planned future possibilities for my life.

My game plan for my life was to be my best and work for my family. I would be taken care of forever. School fees, allowances, salaries—everything until that point—had always been provided to me by my father. I was my father's princess. The apple of his eye, his pride and joy.

My dad was *amazing*; he was a visionary. He was a loving doting father. He put us all through good schools and did whatever he could to provide us a great life. He had big business deals and then he had bust business deals. We had our ups and we had our downs.

My dad believed in himself.

My dad told me a story about the most powerful Chinese words he ever heard. When my dad was a budding entrepreneur, my grandfather said to him, "你 做 得 到."

你 you

做 do/work

得 obtain/get/possible

到 reach

Independently these four characters are simple, yet the combination of the four when delivered encompasses unwavering faith and belief that "you" can do this. In modern day vernacular, the equivalent of 你 做 得 到 is: "You Got This!" My grandfather's words fueled my dad to achieve his first big break.

My father never doubted his ability to spring back from anything. He would never give up. If there were any setbacks in a project, he would say, "Okay, now is the time to retreat and re-strategize so that we can re-launch."

When we had virtually no business, no customers, no

clients, and no meetings, my father would take us to open house events of huge luxury homes. He would take us to showrooms for luxury automobiles and allow us to sit in the different models and accompany him on test drives. He would take us to different trade shows at exhibition halls. He would spend hours talking to us about his big dreams and all the wonders we all could live and experience together.

That was my dad.

In 1999, we were on the brink of bankruptcy. At one point, we were so broke that we were counting our pocket change to make sure my brother and sister had school lunch money. My dad never gave up. He kept on fighting and looking for opportunities. He kept on working on possible deals. That very same week, he closed a million-dollar deal. By 2004, we were once again living in a large luxurious 5,000-square-foot home with two cars, a chauffeur, and housekeepers. My dad showed me the magic of being a phoenix.

"Stace," he told me, "Aim high. Dream big. Never give up. Always keep on walking."

Dreaming BIG was a characteristic and value my father drilled into us.

Before the news of his cancer, I planned everything. I was a total control freak. I had planned my entire lifetime. I planned when I would finish my MBA, when I would meet the love of my life, when I would get married, what our wedding would be like, how many children we would have, and at which age I would give birth to each of our children.

At every single milestone, I saw my father.

I always planned that life would be my dad and me, side-by-side, building our empire, because I was the *best* personal assistant/right-hand man in the world. I was my father's lieutenant.

你 做 得 到 (YOU GOT THIS)

The saddest moment was realizing I could not have those moments with my father. I felt lost and hurt. I was mad at myself for having the audacity to plan such a beautiful life.

My father battled cancer for three years. In that period, we moved from Bangkok to Hong Kong so he could enroll in a university clinical trial using stem cells to treat Multiple Myeloma. My father truly believed he would become that rising phoenix one more time.

Unfortunately—this time around—being a phoenix was not in his cards.

❧ • ❧

Perhaps the biggest casualty of my father's cancer and eventual passing was the death of my vision, hope, and passion.

I became a zombie.

I went to work, ate food, sometimes hung out with friends, slept, and repeat. Work. Food. Socializing. Sleep. Repeat. Every day, every moment was about just going through the motions.

I had been my father's apprentice since I was 14 years old. He trained me how to be a successful respectable responsible entrepreneur. Immediately after his passing, however, I could not face running my family business.

In those years, just seeing my dad's handwriting would make me choke up and cry. It killed me not to be working on our business; but without my dad, I did not know how to show up in the business world. I always viewed myself as the supporting cast, not the star.

I did not have the heart nor the passion to revive our family business, so I did the best I could do to earn money to support my family and that was private tutoring. I taught one-on-one private coaching lessons for subjects like Business Studies,

Economics, Mathematics, and SAT Test Prep to high school students. My students bring so much joy in my life.

My big breakthrough happened when I hit rock bottom after three years of living in zombie mode. I was incredibly proud of my students—seeing my them graduating high school, moving on to university, starting their lives—I felt left behind. They were moving ahead by leaps and bounds and conquering the world, whereas I was stuck in the mud.

That awareness brought several months of total despair that was irritating and painful because I *knew* I had to keep on living. I *knew* I had to force myself to get out of bed and as my father always taught me, *"Just keep on walking!"*

However, *'keep on walking!'* just took way too much energy.

On the second anniversary of my father's passing, I could not get out of bed; I could not manage taking even a sip of water. That was June 24th, 2013. On June 25th, 2013, I had to teach a student who lived two hours away from my home. That student was bright, happy, and enthusiastic about achieving her goals. I knew I had to show up for her because that was my commitment: to prepare her to excel on the SAT. I could not get out of bed for myself, but I made myself get out of bed for her.

That two-hour journey was hard.

Throughout the whole commute I kept telling myself, *"left foot, right foot, left foot, right foot."* I knew I had to take that journey one step at a time. As my father taught me, *"Keep on walking. Tomorrow is another day, never say die!"*

Step by step.

Just kept moving. Just kept walking.

Through this, I learned that tiny steps add up to big steps. Infinite steps mean distanced covered. Just keep on moving.

※ ※

Change happened when a close friend attended an Access Consciousness® class. She learned of a healing technique called *Access Bars®*. My friend gave me a session as a gift.

After the session, I felt different.

To this day, I cannot pinpoint exactly what I felt different about. I dug further by watching YouTube videos (of Access Consciousness) and exploring Access Consciousness materials online. I went on Amazon and bought and read sixteen of the books before attending my first class! I enrolled in a four-day workshop titled, "The Foundation." At that time, the course fee was relatively hefty for me—$1,400. However, I knew I needed to get the necessary tools to recreate my life. So, I saved up the money for the class. In the end, someone 'paid it forward' and I received the workshop as a gift. How does it get any better than that?

By day three of the course, I was not feeling much of a shift. That was the moment I forced myself to get uncomfortable, be vulnerable, and really look at what was working for me and what was not.

The biggest breakthrough I had was learning I did not need to be the provider. I did not need to take on my father's role. The act of "taking care" of everyone was in fact crippling my family. I was being the superior asshole who thought I was the only one who could earn money. I never gave my siblings a chance to stand on their own feet and support themselves.

For several years, many friends and family members had encouraged me to stop looking after my family and start focusing on *my* life. It hurt me every time I heard the words: *'Stop providing for your family. You are not your father.'* I worried,

"How could I abandon ship? How could I be so selfish? What is the meaning of life if not providing and taking care of my family?"

What I realized is that choosing to be a provider was never a position my family imposed on me. It was a role I "bravely" took on because I thought it was my responsibility to do so.

The idea that I could choose for myself and live my own life was scary. I never had made myself a priority in my life. Coming out of that four-day workshop, I felt like I was embarking on a journey to an uncharted frontier. I felt so lost. I did not know in which direction would I go?

"Stacy, what if your vision is not clouded and murky? What if instead you have a whole sky of infinite possibilities ahead for you? You have no more anchor points and you are totally free to choose anything you would like. In this case, what would you like to create?" Dr. Dain Heer, co-Founder of Access Consciousness, encouraged me in one class. In other words, Dain gifted me with an illuminating perspective: I had a blank canvas in front of me.

In another class, Gary Douglas, the Founder of Access Consciousness, gave me valuable advice:

"Stacy, go back to the basics. What do you love? Start from there. Spend time observing people, and if you see anything you'd like to have in your life, start asking for similar."

So that is what I did. I spent time reading books, studying the lives of iconic people, meeting and speaking with people from all walks of life. After a while, I had an idea of the life I would like to create. Within 18 months, my whole financial reality changed: I built two new businesses; I became a Certified Facilitator with Access Consciousness, and I traveled to different cities to teach "Five Days of Change" workshops. It was amazing. Furthermore, my relationship with my body changed so my health made a big turnaround too.

From this breakthrough in my life, I learned *we* give our lives meaning. Life can be meaningless or it can be meaningful. It is up to each of us to discover what meaning we pour into life. What would be fun to create? What would make life worthwhile? If there were absolutely no limitations, what wildest inconceivable dreams could we make real?

When my dad was in the ICU ward, I excused myself and went out to the hallway. I sat on a chair. Broke down and cried. I could not let my dad see me like that because I thought I had to be strong and positive in front of him. To my surprise (and horror), while I was crying, I saw my dad walk out dragging along his IV machine—he was looking for me! He was shocked to find me crying.

He sat down beside me and asked me why I was crying. *"Is it because you are worried I'm going to die?"*

I guess he knew me too well.

"I don't know what to do," I told him. "I don't know what to do if you go."

Foolishly, I was crying about him as if he already died—even though he was right in front of me. He pulled me in close. Locking eye contact with me, my dad took my hand gave it a firm reassuring squeeze and spoke.

"Stace. 你 做 得 到, " he said.

I was too grief-stricken to appreciate the gift he gave me in that tender moment. As if he was passing on the baton: those words were meant for me from now on.

你 做 得 到

(You can do it.)

我 做 得 到

(I can do it.)

I can do it.

I got this.

And I am doing this.

Now that I have achieved success, I understand why he said those words. He had always treated me as a princess, provided for me, looked after me. I had no inkling as to what I could truly do on my own. I always thought life would be handed to me on a beautiful platter.

Right now, my life *is* on a platter—a platter designed, prepared, and cooked by my very own hands.

And what a beautiful platter it is.

Biography

Born in Montreal, Canada, Stacy had a nomadic upbringing. As the daughter of a serial entrepreneur, she grew up and went to school in Hong Kong, Bangkok, and Singapore.

Stacy graduated with the Top Student Award and First Class Honors from the Manchester Business School where she obtained a Bachelor of Science (Hons) in Management, and she has a Bachelor of Science (Hons) from the London School of Economics in Accounting and Finance.

Stacy finds teaching to be an absolute joy. She tutors her students in academic subjects and teaches them strategies and skills to help them master subjects and gain lifelong confidence. She also teaches life tools through various workshops, empowering people to realize they can create the life of their dreams.

Stacy is very involved in community service and is an active member and Past President of her Rotary Club and Guider for her Brownie Unit. She resides in Hong Kong.

Contact Information:

Email:

stacy@stacyho.tv

Facebook:

www.facebook.com/stacyho

Instagram:

www.instagram.com/stacy_ho

Websites:

www.stacyho.tv

www.sheroesclub.com

www.improveyourgrade.com

CHAPTER NINE

Making A Difference Within

Jerome Redd

I was not supposed to make it. I was not expected to succeed. I was a typical, inner-city African-American boy growing up in Baltimore, Maryland, from a poor family with eleven kids. I did have a huge advantage over many other kids in the same situation, though—my parents took us to church, taught us manners, and made education a priority in our home.

When it came to the streets, they told us to stay out of trouble and do the right thing. Ours was a tough neighborhood, overrun with drugs and shootings. It was easy to become the culprit or the victim, and hard to stay in neutral territory. I didn't know how to cope with such a negative environment, so I kept my mouth shut and did my best to stay out of trouble. I tried to hide in plain sight.

My self-esteem and self-worth were so low that every morning I'd look into the mirror and say my version of a daily affirmation, "Hey, monkey, you sure are ugly. Who would want to be around you or go with you?"

I managed to hide in plain sight until the sixth grade, when I met Mr. Posey. He was not just any teacher, he was very,

very special. Mr. Posey was not just an educator, he was an immolator. He did not just speak it. He lived what he spoke—and he did not stop there. Mr. Posey was a man on a mission to change young people and their lives.

I was very fortunate to be there at such a critical time in my life and be a youth under his guidance. I had no idea what he was up to or what I was in for. When I arrived in his class, I thought he was just another teacher in the Baltimore school system. I figured, just like with previous teachers, I would just hide in plain sight. I was stunningly misinformed. Mr. Posey was not having it, on any level. He knew his students between the ages of eleven and thirteen were not only wrestling with the academics, but also with the onset of puberty and adolescence. He had his hands full and he was truly up to the challenge.

Mr. Posey was imposing; he stood about 6'4" and weighed at least 250lbs. His hands were three times the size of ours. At times, he seemed larger than life. Still, you never felt overwhelmed when he stood and spoke to you.

He had certain standards which he followed and expected his students to follow. One was simply basic hygiene, the care of our teeth, hair, and body. Mr. Posey did not hesitate to impose a penalty when we did not live up to his standards. He was not arbitrary—we had three chances, and he would give us two warnings. The third time, he called us out by name and we would suffer embarrassment in front of our class. Mr. Posey was an equal opportunity enforcer when it came to embarrassment.

The time finally arrived for me to take the spotlight. I was not particularly consistent about combing my hair, and he had already given me the usual two warnings. I was disheveled and uncombed for the third day in a row, yet somehow I was surprised when Mr. Posey walked up behind me and placed his hands on both of my shoulders. "Class, Jerome doesn't like to comb his hair in the mornings."

I was more than embarrassed. I was mortified. I was heartbroken. Mr. Posey's opinion of me mattered, and I cared what my fellow students thought of me, too. Even a boulder would not have been big enough for me to hide under.

You might be wondering, "Did Mr. Posey really get your attention?"

I will answer it this way: He never had to put his hands on my shoulders again.

Although his methods hurt, they were very effective. Mr. Posey knew how to compel us to change our mindset and behavior, learn to set goals, and create a plan for achieving those goals. He shook up our lives, and he helped us realize there were different ways—and better ways!—to get a project done.

Mr. Posey's ways and methodology superseded ours and we knew it. Not only did we know it, we embraced his ways, and they felt good.

One of Mr. Posey's amazing attributes was that he not only saw what was on the surface, he always saw beyond the façade.

I made a valiant attempt to continue to hide in plain sight, which had been my successful coping mechanism for 12 years. Mr. Posey was not having it. At every turn, he challenged my very paradigm and forced me to face what I had hidden or tried to hide.

On one memorable day, he was reviewing math with the class. He had given us five math problems to do, and we were expected to answer and show our work. As he walked around the room, checking on each student's progress, he noticed I was sitting there quietly, doing nothing, and he struck.

"Why aren't you doing the assignment I just gave you?"

"I am finished," I replied—quietly—because I could barely breathe.

He surveyed my work and concluded I had done everything correctly, then he uttered two words that would change my life forever: "Help her."

"*Excuse me?*" I said.

He said it again. "Help her."

And I did. This act was transformational. In one moment, Mr. Posey confirmed I had something worthwhile within me and it was worth sharing with someone else. He knew I was plagued with low self-esteem and low self-worth, and he challenged my view of myself.

Mr. Posey later told me I could be anything I wanted to be in life. My crazy self actually believed him.

Until the fateful day I met Mr. Posey, I had given up on life and on ever becoming a man of substance. My tough, giant angel/teacher believed in me when I did not believe in myself. What truly amazes me are the methods he used to reach me and so many others just like me.

Before Mr. Posey, I was doomed. I had been labeled a loser, and I had believed it.

When I got older, my father and brother sneered at me, "You think you're better than the rest of us."

I responded honestly, "No, that's not the truth. I just want to *be* somebody."

I did not want to let my environment determine my outcome in life. Once Mr. Posey planted the seed of positivity within me, I knew nothing could stop me—except *me*.

Though Mr. Posey was extremely helpful, I knew there still

were some skeletons in my closet I had yet to face. I discovered it would not be long before I needed to confront those hidden demons.

After graduating from high school with honors, I went on to college. My winning streak stopped suddenly; my grades were below average and I was struggling, even though I thought I was academically prepared. Before I wasted too much time, I admitted to myself I was not ready or mature enough for a four-year college. I believed the Army would give me needed discipline and an opportunity to go to college part-time, so I signed up.

Soon after I got to my first duty station, I unearthed a painfully astute insight into the person of Jerome Redd.

One day, I entered the military chapel and started looking around. The chaplain, a major, came over and asked, "May I help you?"

I brushed him off politely, "No, thank you. I'm just looking around."

After about ten minutes, he approached me again. "Are you sure there isn't anything I can help you with?"

"No, thanks. I was raised in church back in Baltimore, and I just wanted to see what a military church looks like."

The major said, "Tell me a little about yourself."

I proceeded—or at least I thought I had proceeded—to tell him my story.

To my shock, he interrupted me. "I know what your problem is. You don't like yourself."

"I beg your pardon! I *do* like myself."

"No, you do not, and let me explain why," he replied.

I listened to him repeat, word for word, what I had just said. He was right. I was living up to others' expectations of what I should be, not my own expectations. I was a people-pleaser. I needed the validation of others to exist.

When I realized he was right, at first, I started to cry, and then I got angry. I cried because he was right. I got angry because how in the world did this man, an Army officer I had never met before, know more about me than I knew about myself?

It made me angry. It pissed me off. I promised myself I would never be sideswiped like that again. I would be more self-aware in the future, and I have been.

It took me a while to fully unwrap the chaplain's insight and apply it to myself. Mr. Posey had done a good job of teaching me I had value and what I had was good enough to share with others. It was a huge positive, but upon deep reflection, I knew it was not enough.

I finally understood I knew how to please others, but I did not know how to love myself.

I was stunned. All these years, and I had yet to learn how to love "me."

This life-changing discussion happened when I was nineteen years old. While it took a few more years to get where I wanted to, I have made progress. Between Mr. Posey on my brain and a lot of self-talk, I am now crazy about this guy called Jerome Redd.

If people do not tell me how great I am daily, I tell myself. That's right. I said it. If you have not gotten to know who and what Jerome Redd is and is all about, you are missing out on an awesome treat.

Fast-forward a few years. Thanks to Mr. Posey and the major at the army chapel, I had both a successful military career and a successful time learning to love myself.

After I retired from the Army, I learned a boot camp in

upstate New York was looking for ex-military personnel to be staff members. The camp was for teenage boys ages 12 to 18 who had been pulled into the criminal justice system. Many were from the same inner-city background I'd come from, and they had faced many of the same obstacles and pitfalls.

The young men would spend six months in the upstate boot camp and six months in a non-residential After-Care program in New York City. If I took the job, I would work with them for the first six months of the program.

Here was the opportunity of a lifetime. Who could better reach out to these boys and bring about a change than someone who had already walked the same path the boys were walking? Believing I *could* make a difference in these kid's lives and *could* give back, I took the job.

All too soon, I was quickly reminded of the old saying, "Things are not always as they appear." Important information had not been disclosed to me from the onset. Although I became disappointed in the leadership of the facility, it was not enough to deter my commitment to make a difference in these children's lives; they still needed help and I believed I could help them.

When I looked at these kids, I saw my sixth-grade self. I also saw myself as their Mr. Posey. And just as he did not give up on me, I would not give up on them. What the state required I teach them, I did. I also realized the official curriculum would not reach them on the inside and bring about a change.

On my own, I took every opportunity to share Mr. Posey's philosophy. And guess what? His philosophy still works.

I made it perfectly clear to the boys I was not there to tell them what to do.

"I am here to do two things and two things only," I told them.

"I am here to share information with you and make you think. *That is it.* If I tell you what to do and you go back to New York City and fail, you get to blame me. If you come up with your *own* game plan and go back to New York City and fail, you have no one to blame but yourself. It will not be that you planned to fail, but that you failed to plan. So, what is your game plan?"

Too many of these kids did not have a game plan until they ran into me. I made it perfectly clear: *If you do not have a game plan, someone will give you one. Trust me.*

Once the young men understood what they had done in the past was not working, they were very open to listening to what I had to say. I made it very clear to them if they did not have their own game plan, they were nothing more than an accident waiting to happen.

It was as if I put the mirror of life in front of them and said, "If you do not like what you see, change it." And I helped *them* change their view. I did not change it for them.

That is exactly what Mr. Posey did for me.

A few months after these kids were discharged from our boot camp, I started receiving phone calls directly from the boys. They reassured me they were not gang-banging, selling drugs, or robbing people anymore. Many said bluntly, "Sergeant Redd, you changed my life."

Boys' relatives began to call me, and in more and more cases, family members visiting the facility asked to speak with me. Parents, grandparents, siblings, and other relatives care for these kids and what happens to them hurts whole families as well as the kids.

I remained in the program seven years, and by then organizational politics were so bad it was unbearable to me and disruptive to the kids.

When I realized the kids' loyalty to me was adding to the chaos and divisiveness, I regretfully resigned. I am still working to help them and others through my writing. Many of our youth today are wrongly considered damaged, broken and without hope, and I know it is not true.

I think of myself as a youth who was helped at a critical point in my life. I consider myself grateful and blessed that Mr. Posey did not give up on me. He changed my life in more ways than he could have imagined.

Are you the person who needs a Mr. Posey of your own?

Or are you the Mr. Posey in someone's life?

Biography

Jerome Redd is a dynamic, master motivational speaker, author, actor, and standup comedian from Baltimore, Maryland, where he grew up in the middle of a family of eleven children. After high school and a brief stint at Morgan State University, Jerome spent twenty-one years in the United States Army and retired as a Sergeant First Class/E-7.

While stationed overseas, he worked with youth groups and taught Sunday School to the local high school students. After the Army, he spent seven years as a boot camp instructor for troubled inner-city youth. He is currently the head instructor for a local engineering firm and speaks all over the United States on their behalf.

After retirement, Jerome returned to the classroom full-time, and graduated with honors from State University of New York with a BS degree in Psychology; he also completed one year in their Master's degree School Counselor program.

Jerome has been mentored and trained as a motivational speaker by Les Brown and Antonio T. Smith, and he is a prolific author. His three-book series, *Fixing The Broken, Without Being Broken*, shares the story of how Jerome was successful in making such a difference in those inner-city kids and how parents, teachers, and coaches can reach struggling youth. He also has published three books of poetry, including two specifically for youth and students. The books are available for purchase from Amazon and on his website.

Contact Information:

Email: jeromeredd7@gmail.com
Website: www.jeromeredd.com
LinkedIn: https://www.linkedin.com/in/jerome-redd-a936b64/
Facebook: https://www.facebook.com/jerome.redd
Twitter: www.twitter.com/JeromeRedd

CHAPTER TEN

Health is your Wealth

Tatiana LaBello

In every country and culture, truly wealthy people wouldn't hesitate to swap their fortunes for a healthy body. Too late, they realize their health is their true wealth, and they've spent years wasting it.

We live in a fast-paced world with a ton of pressure. Every day, we are so busy being pulled in so many different directions that between family, work, community, and other commitments, it's easy to understand why we tend to neglect the most important person—*ourselves!*

As a professional life coach and fitness consultant, I work with many clients who suffer from the three "uns"—unhappy, unhealthy, and unfulfilled.

During the initial consultation process, I work with clients to identify the causes of unhappiness and the symptoms that overwhelm them. We usually find they are attributable to a lack of vision/direction/purpose, self-care, or inner positive dialogue.

Thoughts are *so* powerful.

You're about to learn how the power of your thoughts is the key to successfully achieving a healthy lifestyle and your fitness goals. It's time you take 100% responsibility for yourself, and take control of your own health, body, and attitude.

I was fortunate to grow up in a healthy and very active environment. My mother taught dance and baton twirling; she put a baton into my hand when I was three and said, "Join the class!" I retired with a world champion title under my belt by the time I was nine years old.

My fitness career began early. I was a certified aerobics instructor when I was 14, and by the time I was 19, I was the aerobic director at the prestigious Houstonian Resort & Spa in Houston. I would see the same people take my intense classes day after day, week after week, month after month—why did some people lose weight and totally transform their bodies while others stayed the same?

I began my quest to find out.

What is the missing piece?

I have been in the health and fitness arena for more than 20 years and have invested an equal amount of time, money, and energy into personal growth and development. I have studied under virtually every motivational guru during the last two decades and spent countless hours researching programs, attending seminars, workshops, and conferences.

It took years, but I learned the secret:

Our mindset, attitude, and habits prevent us from reaching our fitness goals.

What sabotages us comes from *within*—emotional eating, having a poor self-image, our self-talk, comparing ourselves with others, letting outside pressures control us, and losing direction of our "why."

When you understand these concepts and apply them to your own life, you will literally begin to transform yourself from the inside out.

I attribute a lot of my success to the four principles I am going to share with you. These principles have helped me win national fitness titles, start my own business, and publish my first fitness book.

I call these principles the Four D's:

Desire

The first step toward attaining your fitness goals is becoming aware of what you want. The desire I am talking about is not just a wish or want, it is something that burns inside you.

Take a minute to assess where you are and where you want to be. Think about what you desire to change physically. Do you want to shed a few pounds? Build muscle? Tone up? Lose body fat? Feel better? Have more energy? The first step to getting what you want is allowing those desires, the ones that are truly inside you, to stir and awaken.

> *Desire is the starting point of all achievement, not a hope, not a wish, but a keen pulsating desire which transcends everything.*
>
> **—Napoleon Hill**

Desire is a powerful key to a successful lifestyle. I know you've heard that before, but slow down and listen to the single most important piece of wisdom I can share with you:

What you think about, you bring about.

When you think continually about things you desire to have in your life, you will develop a pattern that will help you focus on what you want instead of what you don't want. This will channel your energy in the right direction and move you closer to your goal.

If you make this focus into a habit, you are well on your way to mastering your fitness goals. Give your desires room to develop into powerful pictures in your mind. Remember, you can't hit a target you cannot see.

Decision

Decision crystallizes your desires into a vision. It is a fact that positive mental imagery projects a positive outcome. Sometimes desires are still too vague—we want to feel healthier, lose weight, gain muscle.

Take it to the next level by choosing the specific goals you want to accomplish. Transfer those specific goals into detailed and imaginative mental pictures. What do you look like when you've attained your goal? How do you feel now that you're stronger and slimmer? What are you doing now that you're fit and healthy that you couldn't have done before? What clothes are you wearing, now that they fit well and show off your toned body?

Imagine striding down the street, looking slim and wearing flattering brand-new clothes from your favorite store, or slipping into those jeans that you once wore. Envision yourself hanging out at the beach, wearing your swimsuit, glowing with the confidence that covers every inch of you like a spray tan. Envision yourself running the trail at the park with incredible strength and endurance.

Lots of details make your vision become reality. Figure out *exactly* how you want your body to look and feel. Clarity is power.

Keep that picture in your mind. If it slips and you start to focus on fearful and doubtful thoughts, become aware that you are having a negative thought attack. Remember, negative input from the conscious mind results in negative output from the subconscious mind.

That is why reprogramming our thoughts by using totally new and more empowering affirmations is so very effective. Without a statement of belief firmly established in our mind, the subconscious is free to be programmed with outside negative influences.

Your thoughts, good or bad, dictate the life you live. Creating healthy habits starts with being aware of each decision we make. Evaluating our decisions brings us either closer to our goal or father away.

If you keep believing what you've been believing, then you'll keep achieving what you've been achieving.
—Mark Victor Hansen

Decide to take control of your life, now!

Determination

Having determination to reach your goals means you must first believe you'll attain them. Can you imagine striving wholeheartedly toward something you don't really believe will happen? Of *course* you'll become discouraged and lose faith.

Determination comes from having the conviction and unwavering belief your goals are within your reach and will be achieved. Meditate on your fitness vision and have faith that you will experience it. "What the mind can conceive the body will achieve."

> *The difference between the impossible and the possible lies in a person's determination.*
>
> **—Tommy Lasorda**

Why is the gym packed in January, but in March it is empty? Focus, vision, and motivation were lost. Be determined to stay the course and not let anything get in your way. Continue to ask yourself: *Is what I am doing now taking me closer to my goals or further away?*

Don't make excuses. Feed your faith and let doubt starve to death. My favorite book says "if you have faith the size of a mustard seed, you can move mountains." So, supersize your faith! The beginning of your triumph begins today when you *believe* you are on the path of accomplishing your fitness goals! As your vision solidifies and your belief establishes a new thought foundation in your mind, your determination will push aside past obstacles and propel you to new heights on the road to success. *Remember, it's not a sprint, it's a marathon. Be determined not to turn back and give up. It's a journey and well worth it.*

Discipline

Discipline is the last step toward creating a lifestyle you love. Don't cringe; reframe your understanding of the concept of discipline. Discipline is *not* punishment being imposed by someone else; it's just inspired action.

When you have specific goals and an exciting vision of where you're going to be, taking action is exhilarating! Not because it's always easy, but because you know that each productive thing you do or don't do is bringing you closer to becoming who you want to be. Everything you are today and will ever accomplish is determined by the habits we cultivate.

Goals + habits + action = results.

Discipline is doing things even though you don't feel like doing them. Small disciplines repeated over and over reap multiple rewards.

Boxing champion Muhammad Ali said it best: "I hated every minute of training, but I said, 'Don't quit. Suffer now and live the rest of your life as a champion.'"

When you are resistant to something, that's when you need it the most. Persistence breaks resistance. Break through the barriers that hold you back. Research shows that progress can be increased by more than 50% when you supplement your activities with concentration and visualization.

Successful men and women from all walks of life are empowered to live out their commitments because they have a burning desire to attain and achieve their goals which come from within. Ali trained with perseverance because his vision of Being the Champion provided motivation for overcoming negative, pessimistic resistance. Ali also believed and affirmed one thing, which is what he eventually became best known for:

"I'm the greatest!" His perception became his reality.

Within our thought process, we plant and water the seeds that bring our dreams and goals to fruition.

Just as a dream by itself will produce few results, actions without dreams to inspire them mostly miss the mark. By balancing the Four D's—Desire, Decision, Determination, and Discipline—you are mixing the essential components to live a lifestyle of power, strength, vitality, and confidence.

Action Steps

- Start with a three-to-five-minute meditation/visualization of your goals
- Write down your fitness goals on a 3x5 index card
- Write one power affirmation statement on the other side of the card
- Carry the card with you and read it three times a day.
- What action can you take *today*? Go do it!

How would your life be different if you operated from this framework in all areas of your life?

>•<

Let's also talk about how these concepts apply to your looks as well as your health and fitness. *This* is where I had my personal breakthrough.

I practically grew up onstage, competing when I was just five years old in baton twirling, modeling, and beauty pageants, eventually competing in the fitness competitions, as I mentioned earlier. Everything was all centered around my exterior, my outward appearance. I was always focused and concerned about the way I looked and I spent a lot of time trying to look and be perfect.

I moved to Hollywood to pursue my dream of acting and modeling. I got wrapped up in the "scene," and became a puppet on a string. Agents, managers, casting directors, all dictated what I was supposed to say or not say, how I was to dress, how I should act and who I should be to book the gig. I slowly lost myself as insecurities and comparisons started to overtake me. I was so focused on the outside, I allowed complete depression to creep up on the inside.

The more I tried to please the people upon whom my career depended, the more lost and disconnected I became. My world became lonely, empty, and unfulfilling. I acted as though I had it all together, but the truth was I was dying on the inside.

I had lost my way.

You may not live in Hollywood, but many of the same pressures apply, especially when you apply them to yourself. When you look in a mirror and compare your image to what you see on magazine covers or celebrity social media, you are comparing yourself to the most glamorous one tenth of one percent of all good-looking people in the world—and it's not even what they really look like. They live a false reality because the photographs we see have been edited, tweaked, and manipulated.

When we let go and stop trying so hard to be what others want us to be—and let go of comparisons—we free ourselves to just be the best version of what we really are.

My true breakthrough came when I discovered that when

we finally take off our masks, get real and are authentic and vulnerable, we connect with others and give them permission to do the same. This may seem confusing, but it's a sign of strength and power.

Honoring ourselves and finding the way to listen to our inner voice is beautiful. Giving to yourself is the greatest way to give to others. You cannot give away what you do not have.

It took a while, but I eventually redefined my definition of beauty: *Real beauty has intangible qualities: self-acceptance, confidence, gratitude, joy, and happiness.*

Being true to who you are is the best way to project your personal image of beauty.

Inner beauty is in *outward* actions. Beauty is making a difference in someone else's life, straight from the heart and not for personal gain.

Make time to replenish yourself so you have something left to give to others. Here are the guidelines; I practice them daily:

- *Consciously practice self-love.* Journaling helps bring clarity to your thoughts and feelings. Look in the mirror and tell yourself, *I love you! I am beautiful! I am bold! I am healthy!*
- *Take time for yourself.* Find ways to spend your downtime that will replenish, refresh, and fill up your cup.
- *Spend time in gratitude.* This is great for your health as well, because it reduces stress and boosts your immune system. Take a personal inventory, a self-gratitude list. Write down three things every day for which you are thankful.
- *5-minute journal.* Download this great app; it sends you daily affirmations, sets morning and evening notifications, and you can journal with it.

- *Celebrate all your small accomplishments.* This was a big shift for me. Prior to learning this, I would look at everything still on my to-do list at the end of the day rather than look at everything I had done. Acknowledge your small victories.

Defining beauty is a personal thing, and comparisons are dangerous.

Your healthy, fit, beautiful self is not a figment of your imagination. Replace those old, unhealthy habits that don't serve you anymore and create new healthy choices that lead you to a life of energy, vitality, mental clarity, and happiness.

It's a journey, and it begins inside your mind.

Biography

Exotic beauty and human dynamo, Tatiana LaBello, born in Las Palmas de Gran Canaria, Spain, is a woman who has pretty much done it all: She has acted on the big screen, reported live from the red carpet, hosted late-night fitness infomercials, and co-hosted ESPN's top-rated fitness show, *Flex Appeal*.

As a former competitor, Tatiana has won many beauty pageants and fitness championship titles. She authored the book, *Step-by-Step Guide to Fitness Competition Success*, to give others the insider tips and necessary tools to insure a competitive edge while guiding them to personal success.

Tatiana has been a cover model and featured in over 15 major publications. She is a former professional cheerleader for the NFL Denver Broncos, NBA Houston Rockets, and USFL Houston Gamblers.

Owner of LaBello Lifestyle, Tatiana coaches individuals to live a healthy lifestyle, a life of purpose and passion. An entrepreneur, she also spends her time as a private investigator, spokesmodel, model coach, and beauty, health, and fitness motivational speaker.

Contact Information:

www.labellolifestyle.com

Email: t.labello@yahoo.com

Facebook: Tatianaanderson

Instagram: Tatianalabello

LinkedIn: Tatianalabello

Twitter: Tatianalabello

CHAPTER ELEVEN

Learning the Hard Way

Ralph Harper

I was born in the South, in tumultuous Birmingham, Alabama, in the early 1960s. I lived my childhood in the era when Birmingham competed with Jackson, Mississippi, for the title of ground-zero of racism.

My parents, my nine siblings, and I lived in a small four-room house in Ensley, a small town just west of Birmingham. Erected in a designated flood zone, our brick house was strong enough to withstand the storms, tornadoes, and the guaranteed spring and summer floods. The front yard was just big enough for a few of us to throw a ball back and forth or play "red light/ green light." The back yard was bigger but weedier, and because we did not have a fence, stray dogs frequently visited us.

All twelve of us coexisted with plenty of love in our tiny home. During the day, the front room was designated as our meeting place; at night, it was our parents' bedroom. It was furnished with a sofa bed, a coffee table, two end tables with lamps, and the family television, which sat on a small table in a corner. The aluminum foil attached to the antenna was supposed to enhance the TV's reception; however, a few punches to the side of the unit seemed to work better.

Momma worked at the Catholic church in downtown Birmingham. She took the bus each day and returned home exactly at 5:32 p.m. if the bus was on time. At least one hour before we knew she would be getting home, we were careful to ensure the house was clean and all of our chores and homework were done.

I recall standing outside the house watching for the silhouette of her white uniform dress as she gracefully walked from the bus stop and across the school yard at Councill Elementary school where we all attended. Her presence was my reminder to get my act together. If any of us had gotten in trouble over the course of the day, we were sure to be spanked.

After dinner was cooked and eaten, we all gathered in the front room to share small talk and maybe watch some TV. When night fell, the moment when the bed was pulled out from the sofa converted our living room into my parent's bedroom, it was time for sleep. We kids had a bedroom with two bunk beds where eight of us slept and another small room belonged to my two older brothers.

Our house was not much to brag about; but it was our home. For as long as our parents were alive, we had a lot of love—some of it tough love—and three meals per day. My father, Clyde Harper, was a little laid back. He seemed content to come home from his job at the Post Office, buy a pint, and consume it before he went to bed. He was not the primary disciplinarian in our home; that was my beautiful mother, Mrs. Catherine Louise Harper. My friends in Ensley called her "Miss Hoppa," and they were afraid of her.

One day when I was just eight or nine years old, all notions of momma's fearsome disciplinary tactics were put into perspective and reduced to what I considered a simple slap on the wrist.

On a brisk, sunny Saturday morning around 9 a.m., my close friend Bobby showed up at my house. For a while, we played with a rubber ball in the front yard, throwing it back and forth. Then we decided to take a walk—an ill-advised walk—that turned into an hours-long extended tour of our neighborhood. We never told our respective parents of our plans. We just went on our way and returned about six hours later.

We stopped at Bobby's house first. His mother, Mrs. Murray, came outside and met us on the porch and she was very upset. She screamed and cursed us in between bouts of scolding and preaching about how worried our families and the neighborhood folk were. Finally, Mrs. Murray spoke directly to me. "Ralph—you know better! Catherine is gonna beat your ass when she gets home. Yeah, I called her already."

I was reluctant to face the music when she got home, so I decided it was safer to follow Bobby and his mother into their house. Inside, Mrs. Murray continued with her tirade. Suddenly, she screamed, "Bobby—take off your clothes!"

Bobby started crying, and he didn't move. Mrs. Murray became even more forceful in her tone.

"Boy—*take off your clothes*! I'm *not* gonna tell you again!"

Bobby finally took his shirt off, exposing his skinny torso, and Mrs. Murray told him to lie across the coffee table in front of her. Bobby was reluctant, and his cries grew louder as the tears flowed down his face like water from two faucets. He begged his mother, "Please, mama, I will not do it again."

I was scared and confused, and I began crying too as the scene escalated. Mrs. Murray glared at Bobby.

"Boy, you *better* lay across that damn table like I told you!"

Still crying and begging, poor Bobby slowly followed her instruction and stretched out on his stomach across the coffee table, knees touching the floor. Mrs. Murray, mumbling and cursing under her breath, took a few steps toward an open door, reached behind it, and retrieved a long brown extension cord from the doorknob. As she returned, still cursing, she wrapped the end of the extension cord around her right hand with her left hand.

As Bobby watched her every move, his cries escalated into horrifying screams.

Then the unthinkable happened. Mrs. Murray, a tall and powerful-looking woman, drew her arm back, and, seemingly with all her might, whipped her son on his naked back with the extension cord.

The screams from Bobby's mouth were unlike anything I had ever heard before in my life. I had never been so terrified. As Mrs. Murray drew her arm back again to administer the second lash, I could no longer bear being there another minute to witness Bobby's brutal beating.

I ran away as fast as I could, and I didn't slow down when I hit the front door. I did not touch the steps as I shot right off Mrs. Murray's porch.

I was in full stride, running because I felt my life depended on it. My hands were like blades, cutting through the air. My thumbs were pointed straight up to the sky; my head was tilted back with my nose pointed upward at a forty-five-degree angle. I was flying and I never looked back.

When I turned the first corner at full speed, I experienced a sense of solace in my heart. I was headed home, and I knew my punishment would not be anything like what I had just witnessed at the Murray house.

Today, that experience, that imagery, those sounds of screams, the tears, and that level of so-called "tough love" serve as the foundation for my belief that certain ills of slavery were passed down from the 1860s and may still be with us today. In my childhood, beatings far too often replaced structured discipline, teaching, and planning for the future.

In my case, when speaking of planning for the future: I was too busy trying to be Super Fly to think about *my* future when I was in high school. Oh, I worked; I started working at Prince Hall Apartments when I was a freshman. On occasion, I even gave momma a little cash to help with the bills.

However, I spent almost all the money I made on cheap clothes and shoes. I guess I wanted to feel like I was somebody important. I wanted to be noticed and popular. I wanted to be the "somebody" our elderly neighbor, Mr. Joe, had told me I would be someday.

When I graduated from high school, I was planning to attend Talladega College, but then I had a rude awakening. Even though I had worked steadily for four long years, all the way through high school, I was flat broke. I was broke because I consciously made bad choices and misused the money I made. I had no one to blame but myself.

Somehow, through the strength of my mother, the support of my father and my siblings, and a nudge from my high school biology teacher, Mr. Samson Julius Bennett, I was able to turn my life around and enroll at Talladega College, a historically Black college started in 1865, majoring in business administration with a minor in computer science.

During my junior year, I was selected for a summer internship at Equitable Life Assurance Company in New York City. The flight to New York was my first, and the experience of being in Midtown Manhattan was quite a cultural shock to a small-town Alabama student, yet I thrived on the experience.

Whoever oversaw the company's internship program was remarkably wise and very aware that small-town youngsters on their own in New York City for the first time could use some security and structure in their off hours. The company assigned me to a four-man dormitory suite at Columbia University, and my stay on campus was a major highlight of my internship (and most probably kept me out of quite a bit of trouble).

At the end of the summer, I returned to Talladega College to finish my studies. When I graduated, I was discouraged by a series of disastrous interviews for jobs in my home town, so I was surprised to learn the folks at Equitable Life were still interested in a Southern boy with a funny drawl. They wanted me to return to New York full-time; I was happy to return and relieved to spend the next eight months safely back in the Columbia dorm as I assimilated to city life. My next safe shelter, as I continued to save money for a place of my own, was staying for a while with the parents of a good college friend.

Figuring out how to survive and thrive in New York led me to my first venture into entrepreneurship.

I was dating a beautiful woman from Belize who loved to dance, especially on the Circle Line's jazz trips. Their boats circumnavigated the island of Manhattan, offering great music and a phenomenal view, but the rides were not cheap and I knew I couldn't afford to take my girlfriend as often as she liked. When I figured out I could charter the entire boat for $3,200 and I could sell tickets and keep the difference, it was a win-win opportunity. Each time I chartered the boat, I netted close to $8,000 profit and helped jumpstart my New York future.

After two years at Equitable Life, I landed a job at PepsiCo in White Plains, in suburban New York. I started at PepsiCo in an Information Technology Analyst role and worked on the national IT network infrastructure. Before I left, I managed some very large national projects, some with budgets in the tens of millions of dollars.

PepsiCo has an unshakable commitment to diversity and inclusion, and I did my best to support its progressive policies. I hired a variety of people, often people like me. After thirteen years, I transferred to Plano, Texas, to work at PepsiCo's Frito-Lay division, where I continued to manage national projects.

In 2001, I left PepsiCo to start my own company, DPLOYIT Staffing. DPLOYIT has been good to me and our employees. Over the years, DPLOYIT Staffing has placed thousands of employees and generated tens of millions of dollars in revenue in the process.

I am still CEO at DPLOYIT and the principal owner. But that is not enough for a full life.

Despite my perceived success, I know I failed in many ways. I failed because I was forced to learn the hard way—on the go and by chance, sinking while I learned to swim. No one ever gave me the answers to the questions I did not know yet to ask.

A few years ago, I had my eureka moment when Pastor Edwards of One Community Church in Plano, Texas, covered "purpose" over a month-long series and I finally discovered my purpose in life.

My purpose in life is to give this generation of our children the answers up front—early in their lives when it will make a difference for their future.

Since its birth, our country has missed the mark in terms of assuring children across all racial and socioeconomic groups are equipped with the skills and values they need to succeed in the United States. The issue has been perpetuated by two unsustained factors: finances and accountability.

One of the best examples of unsustained financial support is the digital divide impacting children in low-income families—the millions of children who have little to no access to technology.

When it comes to accountability, we can no longer ignore parents' unwillingness to properly prepare and guide their children; their unwillingness to give children the moral, ethical, and disciplinary tools they will need to be happy, functional, and successful adults.

Despite my success in business and my personal life, I know I succeeded only by random chance and lots of luck. This is my absolute biggest regret. If I had been prepared to seize my chances, I could have accomplished so much more! Mentoring would have made a tremendous difference in my life.

My God-driven purpose in life is to ensure children do not miss their chances and their possible successes the way I did. My mission is to ensure millions of underserved children across the United States will learn to live by the following seven **REWARDS** life principles. These life principles are embedded within three broader **WIN** accountabilities:

Workforce Development:

- Reading on a regular basis
- Education as the priority
- Working and appreciating the value of working very early in life

Integrity:

- Accountability for one's choices
- Respect for one's self and others

Next Generation:

- Duty to support the next generation of children
- Saving money and being financially astute

Imagine millions of underserved young children who live their lives according to the REWARDS life principles. When they make it to the 2060s, they will be educated, working, entrepreneurs, wealthy, Fortune CEOs, on corporate boards, politicians, and president of the United States of America. They will be the leaders of this country. So how do we help?

I founded Catherine Harper for Keepers (www.ch4K.org), a nonprofit organization named after my mother that focuses on four pillars: Fatherhood/Family, Mentoring, STEM, and Jobs.

I am a huge fan of Malcolm Gladwell and his "outliers" concept and have adopted his idea of ensuring our proteges will get 10,000 hours of IT training before going to college. I have many ideas on how to track them across several areas and assist them with getting jobs, scholarships, and other concepts.

Ideally, we will have CH4K Mentoring/Technology Centers erected in strategic locations around the country. While we still have work to do, we are growing our mentoring footprint in several cities around the country.

In 2012, I met President Obama at a small business conference at the White House. When I told Valerie Jarrett about my nonprofit and our seven life principles, she suggested that we work with My Brother's Keeper (MBK), a mentoring organization that was part of the White House initiatives. I returned to the White House and met with Broderick Johnson, who heads the alliance, and we are now connected with MBK, which is now part of the Obama Foundation

It is all possible.

So—let's go to work.

Biography

Ralph Harper was born and raised in Birmingham, Alabama, and earned a degree in Business Administration with a minor in Computer Science from Talladega College in Talladega, Alabama. He has held a number of IT leadership roles at Fortune 100 companies including Equitable Life, PepsiCo, and Frito-Lay. Throughout his career, Harper has been responsible for proposing, planning, developing, delivering, and supporting enterprise-wide technologies with multimillion-dollar budgets.

He is currently Chief Executive Officer at DPLOYIT Staffing and Business Solutions, which he founded in 2000. In 2008 and 2014, DPLOYIT was recognized by INC, Magazine as one of the fastest growing companies in the United States.

Ralph is Chairman of the Board and founder of Catherine Harper for Keepers (CH4K), a nonprofit organization which is aligned with President Obama's "My Brother's Keeper" initiative.

A motivational speaker on topics ranging from business strategies to fatherhood and the plight of underserved children, Ralph is also the author of an upcoming book that details a plan to improve our children's life outcomes (the working title is *Own the Change—The Mission to Bring a King's Dream to Fruition*).

Contact Information:

Ralph Harper
PO Box 659
Addison, TX 75001

email: shawn@ralphharper.com

Web Addresses:
Company: www.DPLOYIT.com
Non-profit: www.ch4k.net
Personal: www.ralphharper.com

Instagram: mrralphharper
Facebook: Ralph Harper
Linkedin: Ralph Harper

CHAPTER TWELVE

I AM Alive

Amy Jones

In 2006, life as I knew it was no longer working for me. The verbal, mental, and emotional abuse I had endured during the previous eleven years was finally taking its toll. I was beginning to believe I was crazy; a deadbeat mom who had no value. I was taking multiple antidepressants, sleeping pills and was on the verge of becoming an alcoholic.

Miserable, numb, and traumatized, I was contemplating suicide for the third time, though I knew it was not really the answer. I knew the devastating impact suicide would have on my children. But I also knew I could not continue this pattern of being withdrawn to the point where I did not want to live. I had to do something different.

The first step was to remove myself from my toxic environment. I needed space and time to identify my extremely difficult and emotional choices. I had to contemplate the consequences of the actions and decisions that I had to make, and I knew my world was going to fall apart.

The breathing room I needed came in the form of an opportunity to work in the real estate industry in Mexico in 2006. I was afforded space and time to get clean, sober, and clear on what I needed to do for myself and for my sons. After

I returned to the states, it took me another three years to make the heartbreaking decision to give primary custody of my sons to their father. I also had to reconcile the fact I would have to walk away from everything and begin my life from scratch.

I knew the best choice for my sons was to avoid a bitter custody battle. My hope was they would still love me, have a relationship with me, and someday forgive me. I would not recognize until many years later that this would also take away my ability to nurture them in the way only a mother can. But I had made the choice to live and had to accept the consequences of this decision.

After my divorce in 2010, I hit the reset button and started over. For the next seven years, I invested blood, sweat, and tears in my organizing, staging, and moving business. I was finally gaining the footing I had lost. I was on solid ground that felt stable and consistent. I was making progress. I was healthy, happy, content, and finally, comfortable.

And then everything crashed. For the next 18 months, my world turned upside down, shattered, and broke. This would prove to be the most difficult time in my life, apart from leaving my children.

In January 2017, my relationship with my fiancé abruptly ended. After dating for two years, I was ready to get married and he was not. Although it broke my heart, I knew I had to let him go. I was not willing to invest in us any longer as I had overlooked numerous pink flags along the way. I finally accepted I was more committed to the relationship than he was. I did not allow myself time to explore the deep hurt and betrayal I felt when he immediately starting dating after we broke up. I did not grieve the relationship, just as I would later recognize I did not grieve the end of my marriage.

Shortly after my breakup, the opportunity that I had been

praying for since my divorce happened. I had always wanted my sons to live with me and my oldest son asked to move in. My heart was full. I was ecstatic. It was one of the happiest times of my entire life, though he was going through some challenges in his life and was depressed. Even though I tried to help him, after six months, I realized I could not. He was used to a completely different life and lifestyle than the one I lived. I did my best, but for him, it was not enough.

I was devastated when he told me he had decided to move back in with his father, but I knew it was in his best interest. I felt my heart being ripped out of my chest. I did not allow myself time to grieve the end of this chance. I did not allow myself to feel the open wound nor recognize I was reliving the trauma of the circumstances of the divorce, again. I did not grieve the lost opportunity to nurture my son.

For the next few months, I poured myself into work, working almost non-stop. I was grateful for the numbing distraction I felt from working so hard. I was grateful for the exhaustion I felt at the end of the day. I was so tired I could not think or feel, and that became my routine day in and day out. Any feelings that did come to the surface were quickly placed in a box where I put them into a dark corner of my subconscious. When I started to feel deep emotional pain, I would compartmentalize it and put it away. Over time, I began to recognize this was an unhealthy coping mechanism that would have a serious effect on my well-being.

My heart had been broken twice in six months and my defenses were down. As most of us have, I rebounded into another relationship. My judgment was cloudy, at best, and under normal circumstances I would have recognized the glaring red flags from the beginning. But I didn't and allowed the relationship to continue longer than I should have. It became stressful. I wasn't sleeping and knew this was not a relationship I could continue to invest in. I was giving 90% and I deserve more than that. I began to recognize that I'm too understanding. I want to believe in the best in people by believing they have good intentions; intentions like mine. I see potential where, sometimes, there isn't any and then I get hurt. I'm too patient and too understanding and let the situation go on too long, way past its expiration date.

Still reeling from everything that had happened over the previous eight months, I started experiencing pain in my abdomen in August 2017. The words I dreaded came out of my doctor's mouth, "You have a tumor. It's cancer." He then offered a profound choice, "You can choose to fight the cancer where there will be a winner and a loser, or you can choose to love the cancer because it is part of your body." Over the course of the next five months, I changed my diet, began meditating more, and created a visualization process. Every morning when I went in for my acupuncture session at 4:30 a.m., I would say the following mantra, "This is a *treat* meant for healing." It was a *treat* not a *treatment*. I had to change the course of the cancer by choosing to love it because every single cell of me deserves to be loved. It was hard, but I had overcome so much by this time, I knew I could not give up.

This was also a crucial time in my youngest son's life because he was a senior in high school. It would be the last time he would experience all the activities, events, and friendships formed during his high school years. So, I made the decision to only tell a few friends and family that I was ill, but not my sons. I did not want this to become a worry or a distraction in their lives. After all the disruptions I had caused, I could not cause another one.

I did not want my diagnosis to become an area of focus for others in my life; clients, friends, and extended family. I was not willing to have the diagnosis define me or become the center of discussions. I did not want this disease to take on a life of its own when I was working on loving it out of my body. I continued working my same schedule, not slowing down, and not taking any time for myself because I was so intent on hiding my illness.

To take my mind off the challenges I faced, I decided it was time to finish the book I began writing in 2013, *Better for Being Broken: How to Put Yourself Back Together When Your World Has Shattered*. I made a promise to myself that I would finish and publish the book by the end of 2018. My publisher had encouraged me to tell *my* story, not the story I had been telling myself for the last seven years. *My* story is important. All of us have a story and everyone's story is important. After all I had experienced, I had a right to be heard.

Telling my story gave me a voice. I had to do some deep soul-searching to discover, release, and recognize the heartbreak, the grief, and the choices I made. I did not realize what a significant impact this would have on my life over the next few months.

As I completed chapter after chapter, I began reliving my life: cancer, divorce, judgment, post-traumatic stress disorder, leaving my children, guilt, my dream career that never materialized and having to end toxic relationships with family members. It was tremendously trying and emotional however I knew I had to get through it because it was an important and necessary part of my healing process.

I became so involved with completing this major project and my healing process that I failed to recognize that my business partner and I were drifting further and further apart. We were not seeing eye to eye on important business strategies and I had to determine if we were going to be able to weather the storm. I believe people come into your life for a reason, a season, or a lifetime. I finally accepted my business partnership was only for a season and I ended it.

While I had overcome my third bout with cancer, I was now experiencing further health issues. My doctor discovered damage to my small intestine that was allowing food, waste, and bacteria to enter the bloodstream (also known as leaky gut), and I needed to get it under control as soon as possible or face a high risk of developing cancer again. Overworked, exhausted, and mentally and emotionally spent, I had to do more soul-searching. I could not continue this path of continuing to get sick, hiding my true feelings, and stuffing my emotions down.

During my daily meditation and reflection time, my soul released the answers and insights I needed. I had been hiding behind fear—the fear of addressing the elephant in the room when I was with my sons. I was the person who had caused my children pain; I was the elephant. I was the person who was unable to show up for them time and time again. I was the person who was getting physically ill because I had not addressed the pain I was causing myself by not asking for their forgiveness. I was the person who was not showing up for myself emotionally and I was not able to show up emotionally for my sons, either. I had to forgive myself first, so I could release the fear so that my heart would open and release all the trauma, pain, disease, and illness I was keeping inside.

I had a heart-to-heart talk with my sons and validated the sadness and disruption I had caused in their lives. I acknowledged the choices and decisions I made that they may never be able to understand. I asked for their forgiveness for all the times that I was not present, did not show up, and could not support them.

I promised to be emotionally available for them going forward. I had to get well, not only for myself but for my sons. They lovingly forgave me and I knew this would be a fresh start for a positive, present, and deep relationship. This break through moment helped illuminate an incredibly life-changing and even more impactful break through a few months later.

After our emotional meeting, I accepted I needed some time off to fully recognize, understand, and acknowledge all that had occurred. I had to discover what steps I needed to take to heal and become whole again.

I believe things come full circle and for my healing process, I had to return to the location where my world and my life fell apart: Mexico. Just like I did before my divorce, I had to remove myself completely from my environment to gain perspective and understanding of the circumstances of the last 18 months.

During my three weeks in Mexico, I began to contemplate what had brought me to the point of exhaustion and illness; heartbreak after heartbreak, not allowing myself to grieve, ignoring my feelings, stuffing my emotions, and discounting the experiences and challenges I had been facing.

My reflections brought three things to the surface: forgiveness, fear, and grief. I had not fully accepted the forgiveness from my sons. I had not fully felt the emotional release from our meeting. I had not completely forgiven myself for the trauma and heartbreak I had caused them. I had to forgive myself so that I could heal. I needed to allow their forgiveness to fill my heart with unconditional love because that is what I receive from them.

I had been hiding behind fear for so long it became normal for me. I was fearful of allowing myself to deeply feel. I was fearful of telling my story. I had to accept I could not hide behind the fear of telling my story and still contribute to the world.

Our stories weave a thread of connection between us. Releasing fear allows me to be the lighthouse that I know I am and that I am meant to be. Grief is one of the things that caused my heart to break, over and over. I did not grieve the ending of any of my relationships. I did not grieve the lost time with my sons while they were growing up and after the divorce. I did not grieve the loss of my ability to nurture my sons after the divorce. Not allowing myself to grieve was keeping my heart from healing and becoming whole again. I have accepted that I must grieve and feel my feelings; the deep emotional hurt and pain associated with loss. Grieving helps me connect to myself and recognize I will get hurt but hurt is only temporary.

Reconciling all these emotions defined, transformed, and shaped the most significant and impactful breakthrough of my life: I am alive because of my sons. I chose to get a divorce instead of continuing in a toxic marriage that would ultimately have led to my ending my life. Making the incredibly heartbreaking decision to leave my children, I am alive. I was not supposed to be able to have children due to my physical make-up, cancer, and illnesses however, because of the course of holistic treatments I chose, I was able to have two healthy children despite the odds. I was meant to have children because I was meant to live. The only reason I am alive is because of my sons.

I am alive and can share my story with the intention that it will provide light in the darkness, hope when everything seems hopeless, a different perspective, courage to make difficult decisions and give a sense of empowerment and direction. I have lived in the dark for too long. My break through has allowed my essence to illuminate the darkness to release fear, forgive, grieve, and live in the moment.

Biography

Amy Jones is a personal growth visionary, author, and international speaker who lives and breathes one simple philosophy: *live in the moment.* For more than two decades, she has inspired thousands of people; intent on helping facilitate their personal growth and self-healing process by creating opportunities for significant and lasting life changes.

Amy is a highly sought-after speaker and her series *Getting Rid of Possessions: It's Harder Than You Think* has the highest attendance in the history of the Generations program at Methodist Health Systems. She is the author of *Better for Being Broken: How to Put Yourself Back Together When Your World Has Shattered.*

Contact Information:

Connect with Amy Jones at: www.TheAmyJones.com

CHAPTER THIRTEEN

Get Up! AGAIN!

Toni L. Pennington

Half of surviving is attitude. Unfortunately, it took years before I managed to grasp that concept.

When I had three surgeries for fibroids, I didn't get it. When I thought I was dying and had blood clots in my lungs, I couldn't believe it. And when my test came back positive for HIV, I was completely devastated.

That day I believed my life was over.

My dream of sharing my life with a true partner now seemed impossible. I would never get married. I mourned. I had a bleak vision of growing old, all alone, eating dinner at a long table with a cat sitting on the other end, and it terrified me.

My medical problems started off dramatically, with fibroids "growing like wildfire," as my gynecologist so graphically described them. I was extremely anemic. Sometimes I felt like I was dying. I could barely climb a flight of stairs. I was often afraid that I couldn't make it from one place to the next without bleeding through my clothes. I was embarrassed. Now I realize how ridiculous that thinking was. Why would I be embarrassed for being sick? Surgery was the only option.

Five years later, I was in the same situation. My previous doctor had retired and my new doctor was wonderful. He believed in minimally invasive procedures, but, he was forced to open me up, as had the first doctor. The third time, a sonogram revealed the scarring from previous surgeries and the new fibroids made it impossible to save my uterus. It had to go.

While I'd never yearned for children, once that possibility was taken from me, I felt a loss. I still wasn't married and I had no idea whether someone might come into my life whom I could imagine as the father of our children. But it was what it was. I had the surgery.

When I got past that hurdle, another one was right around the corner. I was lying in bed watching television when I felt like a dagger was ripping my heart out of my chest.

The pain got worse. I'd never felt anything like it. Was I having a heart attack? The shock bolted me into an upright position. It was as if someone snatched the front of my pajama top and sat me up like a puppet. I was stunned. The thump of my heartbeat pounded in my eardrums.

I was afraid, but I couldn't call anyone. I knew they would insist that I go to the hospital and I did not want to go. I settled back against a pile of pillows, afraid to lie prone, praying that I would wake up in the morning. I figured if I died my neighbors would smell my rotting corpse and eventually the cops would break the door down, or my brother or sister would investigate if they couldn't reach me.

My behavior that night was incredibly stupid, but that's what I did.

The following day I went to work as usual. The scare of the previous night crossed my mind, but I ignored it. In the weeks to come, I continued my routines –work, school, rehearsals. I was determined to be who I was before I'd ever been ill, an active, healthy woman.

After six months I was losing my ability to breathe. My decline was slow. I was so busy, I really didn't notice what was happening to my body.

One cold night, I was leaving to go to class. Even though I hate socks and almost never wear them, I was afraid I'd be cold so I grabbed a pair. I sat on the side of the bed to put them on. When I bent over, I lost my breath. Tears welled up in my eyes.

Intuitively, I knew something was seriously wrong with my body. I could no longer deny it. I called a friend and asked her to take me to the hospital.

Both my mother and father died due to heart issues, and I was afraid it was my heart. I had already outlived my mother's short life of 39 years, so I was relieved when I heard the emergency room nurse say, "Pennington's been rejected from cardiac care." I had blood clots in my lungs.

I would never have imagined that my issue would be my lungs. After all, I was a singer. I walked, I danced, I didn't smoke. I didn't do any of the things that I thought could impair them. My visit turned into six days in intensive care and four additional days of the medical staff trying to find the right combination of blood thinners.

After I was released and went for my follow-up appointment, my doctor asked if a student could sit in on my appointment. Always the comedian, I replied, "Of course, I'm interesting." Dr. C. chuckled and the student entered the room.

"Patient was diagnosed with a spray of blood clots in her lungs."

"Wait . . . what? A *spray*? I thought I had like two or three in each one."

"No. You had sprays of blood clots in both your lungs."

I swore I had never heard this. It turned out that a clot had

149

pinched off because of the fibroids and traveled up into my lungs and disseminated. I was one of 13 known cases like that ever. Once my doctor explained the rarity of my case, I asked him if we were going to make any money or at least be featured in JAMA (Journal of American Medical Association).

Sadly, he said no. Oh well. For six months, I had been a walking time bomb. I could have dropped dead in the street.

After the clot episode, I was instructed to go directly to an emergency room if I ever felt anything strange in my chest. Later that same year when I had chest pains, I went straight to the hospital. Tests showed my white blood cell count was unusually high, suggesting my body was trying to fight something really aggressive. When they asked if they could test me for HIV, I said "Of course." I had been tested before and the results had always been negative. I wasn't worried.

Three months passed before I got the results. That day Dr. G told me my viral load was 1,280,000 and my T cells were at 198. Anything less than 200 is considered AIDS.

My immediate thought was that I couldn't tell my brother or sister. This news would destroy them. I went out to my car and sat for a while. I knew, besides living the rest of my life alone, I would never laugh again. That really hurt. I decided that I needed to tell the person I was seeing at the time immediately because I didn't think I would have the nerve if any time passed. I drove directly to his job praying the whole time that I would be focused and not get into a car accident. He wasn't there. Then God blessed me.

As I drove home and stopped at a red light, I heard yelling. I looked around and saw a very small man on a very large motorcycle. The man had his arms stretched up in the air holding onto his super-high ape-hanger handlebars, his cell phone was tucked into a cap under his helmet, and he was yelling into the phone.

So much for my lifetime without laughter. I started laughing, and I laughed for at least five minutes. When I stopped, I thanked God for answering me immediately. I felt as though He said, "I know you just heard something that will change your life forever, but it's not going to be the way you think."

I hadn't lost my sense of humor because I had gotten bad news. Funny things were still going to happen, and I was still going to laugh.

All this is to say, no matter how dark the days may be, embrace the small things that bring you joy. They are small and they are personal. Your pleasures may not be like anyone else's, but if they make you happy, embrace them.

I went home, got in bed and cried. I cried and I cried. I thought about people I knew who were mean, hateful, nasty and downright unkind. Most were married and seemed to have great lives. Why was this happening to *me*? What great sin had *I* committed? I blamed myself. AIDS was the number-one thing I was afraid of and here I was—dying. Not only with a positive diagnosis but with a stratospheric viral load.

But God was still communicating with me.

After I wrapped my mind around my reality, I came back to myself. I recognized that this awful disease was not representative of who I was. It did not wipe away 45 years of life. Everything I had accomplished to that point did not disappear. *I was still me.*

I made the decision to choose life. That day, my doctor gave me a prescription for the medication that I still take today. Within 30 days my viral load dropped to 1800 and my T cells increased to 213. I was not dying.

I have shared my story because I want people to understand that you can choose life.

After three surgeries to remove fibroids and eventually my uterus, I chose life.

After a 10-day stay in the hospital due to pulmonary emboli, I chose life.

After my devastating HIV diagnosis, I chose life.

I knew I had more life to live. I certainly had more to give. There was still a whole world I wanted to see. It may sound as if I'm over-simplifying health issues. I am not. All of my issues have been extremely serious, and two were life-threatening, but I believe that God's plan was to use me.

I thought back to the 1980s when I lost friends to AIDS. When I visited one of them I saw maybe a dozen vials of medication on the table. I peeked at one and the label said Azidothymidine (AZT), which I knew was the drug used to fight AIDS. My friend took over 30 pills every day. They did not save his life. 25 years later I am allowed to live. I take one pill a day.

I don't ask why. I only say thank you. My beloved reminds me occasionally that I am a walking miracle. Sometimes I forget (he'll love reading this).

Half the battle of dealing with life's grief and pain is attitude. You've got to look up. There's nothing below you but the ground—dirt, or worse, cement. Above you is the sky and all possibilities.

Three days after the HIV diagnosis, I went for a previously scheduled biopsy on my thyroid. That was the same day the New York Giants were being celebrated with a parade along the Canyon of Heroes in downtown Manhattan. I told the doctor that my HIV test had come back positive. I could see that he was surprised by my calm demeanor. He asked me to repeat it. I did.

"When did you find this out?" he asked.

"Two days ago."

He stared at me for a few seconds then he covered my hand with his, smiled and said, "You're going to be all right. You know why?"

I shook my head, about to cry.

"Your attitude. Half of surviving these kinds of things is attitude. I'm not going to do the biopsy. Good luck to you."

I threw my hands up and said, "Okay, then I'm goin' to the parade!"

"I wish I could," he said.

We laughed and he disappeared behind the curtain. I got dressed and left. I walked to the train station, squeezed into a sea of blue, surrounding myself with happiness. In spite of what I was dealing with, being at the parade was the best medicine. That day was such a blessing. It was greater than happiness. I was surrounded by pure joy. For a few hours that joy seeped into my soul. It was the beginning of my healing.

Don't get me wrong. I'm not saying that I didn't regress. Remember, the two previous days were spent in tears, bitter tears. I don't remember eating, going to the bathroom—all I remember is tears. But I got up. That was more than a decade ago.

As long as you get up you can win. Always get up. Put one foot in front of the other and begin to move forward.

How do you move forward when you feel defeated? The simple answer is that you push. You push through. I would never suggest that pushing is easy. It is not. If there is anyone on this planet that you love—a sister, brother, parents, a spouse, children, a pet; use them as your guiding light. Push toward them. Let love support you.

Personally, I believed God always told me when to share my story with someone. I shared it one person at a time. Usually, someone chose to confide in me about an extreme trial that they were facing. I did not use my illness to say, "Oh you think that's something? Get a load of this!" Absolutely not! I prayed that sharing my experiences would offer hope.

For people who know me very well, there's probably been no time when they haven't seen me being creative, joking, vibrant and enjoying life. That's how people see Toni Pennington. My fear of sinking into an abyss of depression and mental and emotional paralysis was greater than attempting to make it through another day so I pushed and am still pushing.

My story is not the worst thing that ever happened to anyone, but I've had people say, "Oh, I don't know what I would do."

My answer has always been and will always be, "You'd do what I did. You would ask the doctors and you'd ask God or whoever or whatever you believe in, "What do I do next?" And you'd be here telling me your story. Believe me. I lived it." Some chuckle. Some simply nod as if to say, "I get it." And in that moment I feel that my work is done.

Today, my viral load remains undetectable and my T cells are well above 1000. I am alive. I am happy. I am in love. And I enjoy every day that God gives me.

Biography

Toni Pennington is a Brooklyn, New York native currently living in Jersey City, New Jersey. She holds a Bachelor of Arts degree in English from New Jersey City University.

Although she has been a singer for most of her life, she has found great joy in writing. Toni enjoys her job as an Academic Success Coach and Tutor Mentor at NJCU. She has hosted and participated in several Student Symposiums. She is published in several issues of *PATHS*, one of the school's literary volumes, and is currently working on her Master of Arts degree at Southern New Hampshire University.

Contact Information:

Email: joyforeverenterprises@gmail.com
Website: joyforeverenterprises.com
Instagram: Joyforever1love
Twitter: Joyforever108

CHAPTER FOURTEEN

We Are Unstoppable

Reagan Jasmin

Where I lived, in a depressed, crime-ridden area of South Africa, it was rare to be born into a family in which your mother and father were married to each other. It did not seem like a blessing when I was very young, though, because my father was in the military and stationed away from home most of the time.

After he left the military, my father was unemployed for years and my mother was the sole wage earner. She would return home from her retail job exhausted and frustrated, still finding time and money to bring home a small piece of chocolate candy for me. I was just a child but I could sense the financial pressure weighing heavy on my mother.

Her feet were constantly sore from work and all the walking she had to do—a common complaint among those who lived in our racially mixed neighborhood during the apartheid era in South Africa. I was too young to really experience apartheid, but I did have a taste of it.

Where we lived during the 1980s was infested with gangsterism and drugs. It calmed down during the 1990s and then the violence rose again. Crime flourishes whenever unemployment is high.

When I was six, my parents sent me to live with my mother's family because they believed it would be safer there. My Granny's home in Newlands East was a very Christian environment, with gospel music always playing in the background. The music I heard spoke to me, and it was the foundation for my Christianity. For the first eight years of my life, things seemed to be going well with our family. We did not have much, but it was all I knew.

After my father found a job, my parents moved into their own house in Newlands East. Their work kept them both away from home for 12 hours at a time, so I still spent most of my time with Granny. She was my pillar of strength and the one who raised me.

When I started living with my parents again, my father took his frustrations out on me. He seemed to have two personalities. At times, he was a good person and father. At other times, he had a mean side. Being around him felt like walking on eggs because I never knew which version of him would show up.

When I was twelve, I began seeing more of his mean side. I thought his anger was my fault. If I commented, I was wrong. If I kept quiet and looked away, then I was challenging him. My foundation always had been church, but even that was an issue for my father. It was confusing and stressful. I started to fear him and I was angry. All I wanted to do was to finish school so that I could leave home.

I used to believe my mother was not doing enough to protect me and that angered me more. I needed an outlet and had none. Abusers control the people around them and what they do, and my father was no exception.

I experimented with marijuana because I knew he would be angry if he found out. Marijuana was my escape and rebellion.

Just before my dad would arrive home from work each day, I headed out to smoke with my friends, knowing he would smell it on me when I came home. I eventually moved to harder drugs. I knew he would be angry if he knew I was taking them and that gave me satisfaction. I took drugs to hurt him, not to hurt myself.

One day my parents and I had a massive disagreement and I left home. I was determined to make my parents feel the same pain I felt.

Initially, I moved back to my grandmother's home—my place of refuge—but I left because my parents would know where to find me. I did not know where I was going; I just wanted to get out of their lives.

At the time, I had a weekend job. After work, I walked the streets of Durban all night and then would head back to that job exhausted. One night while wandering, I bumped into a friend of mine, Anthony (Ants) who asked where I was staying. I told him I had no place to stay.

"What do you mean that you have no place to stay?" Ants said. "You can stay at my house, bro."

For several months, I lived at his parents' home. During that time, we were always high, skipping school, and heading down a highway of destruction. But I knew I wanted more out of life.

I was adamant that I was finished with my parents and did not want to see them.

There was a community park where my friends and I used to hang out. Every Friday, my father would finish work at about noon and would drive past. I noticed him, but paid no attention. One Friday, he did not drive past. I figured he must have been working late.

At 3 p.m. that day, I was standing outside my friend's house and my mother and other family members pulled up and asked to talk to me. I got in the car.

"Daddy has passed away," my mother told me and she burst into tears.

I was silent, I did not know what to say or how to feel.

"Why would you lie like that?" I finally asked, confused and a little afraid. "If you want me to come home, just tell me." I could not believe he was dead because he had never been ill. It made no sense.

I went home with my mother and learned she had been telling the truth.

I felt guilty and wondered if my actions had been worth it. All I could remember were the good things about him and regret consumed me. I blamed myself. I thought maybe if I had been a better son instead of being so rebellious, he would be alive. I felt as if I was being buried under layers of negativity.

Eventually I learned that before he died, my father asked my mother for help. "Pray for me," he asked humbly. "I want to give my life to God."

Mother did pray for him. Three days later he passed away. Many people do not have the opportunity to make a breakthrough like that before they die.

After he passed, I looked for every reason to take responsibility for his death. The pain of the loss and the regret was slowly starting to break me down.

When we discovered his death was caused by being poisoned, I wanted to hurt the responsible person. The emotions I was feeling—loss, guilt, anger—were wrecking my brain and my heart. I started hearing stories of how my father had asked about me daily, which shocked me. I had thought he did not care. Could it be he just did not know how to treat me?

Later I learned people who have been hurt tend to hurt other people, and I believe that was the case between my father and me. My father was doing what he knew. Hurting people can be a vicious cycle, but I finally broke it through forgiveness.

My father's brother and I are very close, and he always treated me with love and respect. I could not understand why two brothers were so different despite growing up in the same environment. But both men made different decisions—one allowed their past to make them into a better person and one allowed the past to change them into an angry stranger. Understanding that helped me realize I did not have to fall victim to the way I had been treated; I could be better than that.

My mother's brother-in-law decided I needed a break from everything that was going on, and he said I should visit him in Johannesburg. This uncle always treated me as if I was his own son and I believed he was the type of father I deserved.

My uncle offered guidance, built me up, motivated me, and was a pillar of strength. He trusted me no matter what anyone said. He also believed my father wanted the best for me even though I could not yet see it.

In my uncle's home, I had access to lots of personal development material which played a major role in my personal breakthrough. Those simple yet profound books contained stories that changed my perspective on life.

I focused on God's word. I attended church, and paid close attention to every sermon. I began to feel the preacher talked directly to me, and it lit a fire within me. I started believing I could motivate people. I realized I am a man who can impact people's lives with a story most people *go through* and but many do not know how to *grow through*.

During this period, I learned the power of speaking things into existence, visualization, and the power of the subconscious mind by immersing myself in motivating materials.

I began to realize my father taught me some valuable lessons. I knew that if it was not for him, I would not have been able to handle some of life's challenges.

My father's words often pierced me deeply, but now I know I am the opposite of everything negative he called me.

But my challenges and pain did not end with my father's death.

Two years after my father's passing, I was back visiting relatives in Durban when I bumped into an old friend, Dallin Godfrey, who could relate to me because his dad also had passed away. We were always close, and we were together daily during my visit.

After I was back in Johannesburg, Dallin called and asked me to be his best man for his wedding and to come to his engagement party. The day I arrived, he had an argument with his fiancée and left their apartment without saying anything to me, which was unlike him.

I went looking for Dallin, could not find him, and returned to their apartment to sleep. I woke at midnight and heard his fiancée crying because she was concerned about him. In the morning, we received a call that a body had been found at a nearby school and it might be him.

When I was approximately 300 feet from his body, I knew it was my friend. Anger and shock took over and all I wanted was revenge.

"I should have been with him and maybe he would be alive or maybe we would both be dead, but we would have been together," I thought.

We buried Dallin on the day that had been scheduled for his engagement party. At the funeral, his family reacted oddly toward me, and I learned they believed I had murdered my best friend. I had no clue why, but I did understand people usually need someone to blame.

Dealing with the loss and being accused of murder had me questioning myself again. People asked why, when we always had been together, was I not there—or maybe I had been?—when he needed me most.

I did not have the energy to respond to their accusations.

While the investigation was going on, I stayed in Durban with my aunt and uncle. It was lonely and traumatizing. The murder was eating away at me.

My uncle came home one day and told me I had to leave. I remember walking the streets alone late at night asking, "God, why this is happening? What is the lesson? How can there be a lesson in this?"

I had walked the same routes before, but Dallin always had been with me. Sometimes you must walk alone on a painful path and that is when God will reveal his plan to you. However, if someone had told me that at that moment, I would have thought it was a joke.

I forgave those who accused me and the person who killed my friend. I was at peace and God had my attention and I realized I had no control over what transpired. I could not have saved my friend or prevented his death.

When I was called to the police to identify some items that were stolen from Dallin, I learned the murderer, a male acquaintance of ours, had been apprehended. I was relieved; I had already forgiven him.

Withholding forgiveness will consume you and delay your

breakthrough. During the investigation and trial, I discovered a strength within myself I never knew existed. I learned how the power of decision and the power of forgiveness can heal any person.

Simply forgive.

When we utilize that deeper power inside us all, we are *unstoppable.* Our test becomes our testimony.

I survived this experience knowing bad things may still happen to me and those I love. Yet now I know I am a conqueror, a child of God, and everything that happens to me builds me up into a stronger force that cannot be destroyed.

You can run from adversity or learn from it; if you do not learn, you will be trapped in an endless recycling of the trouble. Tell yourself you can get through whatever it is. Surround yourself with people who believe in you and material that inspires you.

It worked for me and it will work for you.

God's plan is for you to prosper in your life. Sometimes you must overcome adversity to fulfill God's plan and your purpose. Sometimes it is unfair and unreasonable, but these challenges can be the foundation for personal breakthrough.

If you look deep enough, you can find the lesson in every situation. What may seem like a *setback* is a *set-up* for God to bless you.

Your breakthrough is waiting for you and you have a choice: Are you going to receive it? I made that choice. I chose to break the cycle of pain and unforgiveness and build a family bond that is unbreakable.

Biography

Reagan Keith Jasmin is an entrepreneur, international motivational speaker and experienced protection specialist who was brought up in an underprivileged neighborhood in South Africa.

His breakthrough came at a young age while he served as a private military contractor in Iraq. The experience altered his perspective and brought out the purpose of his life, which is to inspire people young and old. Today, he has made it his life's mission to improve peoples' lives by being an example that you can achieve anything in life if you put your mind to it, no matter how tough the circumstances.

Contact Information:

For more information, contact Reagan at:
reaganjasmin@gmail.com
Facebook: Reagan Keith Jasmin
Instagram: breakthruwit_reags
Twitter: breakthruwit_reags

CHAPTER FIFTEEN

Rising from the Ashes

Carol Gockel

She Fell

She fell
She crashed
She broke
She cried
She crawled
She hurt
She surrendered
And then . . .
She rose again

　　　　　—Nausicaa Twila *(Used with*
　　　　　permission from the author.)

The room was dark. I could not tell where I was. I turned my head to the right to open my left eye to get a wider view of my surroundings only to find my eye glued shut. As I pulled my body to turn toward my right, a sharp pain in the back of my neck caused me to bury my face in the pillow once again.

The left side of my body felt numb, I could not feel my arm. I turned slowly onto my back and realized I was naked. Disoriented,

I tried to search the room for some indication of where I was. My fingers felt the linen underneath, a familiar sensation; the air was warm and the scent stale. The ceiling fan was rotating silently above as my mind started to understand: I am on my mattress, I am in my room, and I am still alive.

Tears started streaming from the corners of my eyes once more, uncontrollably like the many times before. My throat, dry and sore, could barely make a whimper. Then came the tsunami of pain pouring out of every inch of my body like hundreds of spikes piercing through my skin at once. I howled in agony as I felt ripped apart from the inside, clenching my fists tightly on my sheets.

Curling myself into a fetal position, I soundlessly wailed in the sparsely furnished room and surrendered to my demise; humiliated, ashamed, discarded, $100,000 in debt, penniless, alone in an apartment for which I could not afford the rent. Feeling worthless, stupid, and used I mourned for the loss of my identity, my life, and a decade of my youth.

⇒• •⇐

I was juggling school with part-time work to make extra pocket money. He was a student at the university where I was working at the bazaar that day. Halfway through my sales pitch at the booth, he gave me his number, invited me to call that evening to speak further, and then rushed off to his lecture.

The boss decided to take us out to celebrate at the hottest club in town for our work that weekend. Eager to close one more sale, I called him to arrange to meet at the club.

He appeared out of nowhere and handed me a glass of Long Island Iced Tea. We chatted. Before I knew it, the entire group of people I had arrived with had left me behind. He offered to drive me home.

I have wondered how my life would have been had I not

accepted that ride home.

Ever since I was a young girl, it had been instilled in me that girls grew up to be married off and become a member of her husband's family. I would bear their name, have children to honor the family, and be cherished by a loving husband for my entire life.

My brothers and I went to a neighborhood school; I was an average student, not particularly bright. My parents' expectations were only that we would score high enough to move on to the next grade. They never pressured us to excel. Life was living from paycheck to paycheck, going through the motions every day—just "being." My father told me to take care of my looks and to stay attractive enough to "marry up" so I would not have to work my buttocks off—to meet someone who would provide for me.

That shaped my idea of what my life role should be: a domestic goddess, loving mother to my brood, living in a nice house, with a husband who'd support us financially. I had a list of criteria for my would-be spouse. He would be:

- attractive, but not overly so,
- successful, or on track to be,
- charismatic,
- devoted to me, and
- dedicated to loving and caring for me forever

And there he was, sitting next to me in the car as he drove me home. He bought the car himself with money he made as a real estate agent while juggling school as a student. He shared his desire to be self-reliant and not ask his father for money. He was a rugby star, yet he exuded a quiet confidence, almost mysterious. He wasn't showy like the boys I'd met from privileged backgrounds.

Before I got out of the car, he asked if he could call to get to know me better. I thought, "He is different. He wants to get to know me for *me.*"

I took the bait.

I'm from what's considered a working-class Singapore family. My mother left school at a young age to help look after her siblings while my maternal grandparents, immigrants from China, toiled hard as manual laborers.

My father came from a middle-class upbringing. He was the youngest of five children, and after high school he went to work in the grocery store my grandfather owned. After my parents married and bought a flat, my mother was a stay-at-home parent raising three children. My dad worked in the entertainment industry, starting his shifts at night, and returning during the day to sleep.

My background could not have been more different from his. Based on our academic achievements, upbringing, and circle of friends, we would never have met were it not for that day at the bazaar. Within months of our meeting, I moved in with him.

Living together is frowned upon in Asian culture—it's a disgrace to the family. But I was head over heels in love with him, and I could not have cared less what others thought of me, not even my parents.

There were only a handful of explosive outbursts during our relationship: throwing a wine glass on the floor, kicking the furniture, breaking a mirror. There was nothing overtly physical toward me that would have made me fear for my safety.

Words were his weapons. It started subtly and innocently—a comment about my clothes, my hair, or my makeup, followed by him scrunching his nose up and shrugging, "Well, it's your choice." He would pass it off as teasing and punctuate his words with a little cheeky laugh.

"That is only expected of you, baby. What you have done is not quite an 'achievement.' I know you can do better," he would tell me in a gentle, yet slightly mocking tone. It was his way of belittling the little triumphs I had worked hard to achieve while disguising his words as encouragement.

I was slowly isolated from my friends because he said they were a bad influence and would hinder my personal growth. I was persuaded to keep my family away, for their working-class status would not go with the image he had carefully created of us.

His cold shoulders, silent treatment, and withholding of affection ebbed away the foundation of my being. He began to often twist his words to deny promises he'd made or words he'd said in the past. I began to question my own reality and sanity.

His verbal attacks escalated over the years.

Many times, he would give me positive reinforcement only to tear me down, telling me I could be worthy if I just changed my bad personality traits. If anything were to go "wrong" in our relationship, he told me, it would be because I had not heeded his advice or sought his approval before acting.

That was how he exerted control over me. His look of contempt, disgust, sadness, and disappointment combined with his voice and tone always made me feel terrible. I was chided until I conformed to his wishes.

There was no shouting from his end, only from mine. I had to defend myself. My words and my beliefs were begging to be heard. I was angry, frustrated, despondent, and constantly in tears. In his response, he would say in the calmest voice imaginable that I was acting emotionally and irrationally, and if I changed my ways, that would not happen in the future. In a very literal sense, I was a baby for him to mold the way he deemed fit, demeaning me whenever he could and masquerading it as love.

Why didn't I leave? It's hard for those outside our relationship to see the damage within. To outsiders, we were successful and happy. In reality, I was profoundly depressed and had lost whatever self-confidence I'd ever had.

To make it even harder for me to leave, he made sure I was at the mercy of his financial control over my earnings. For the entire thirteen years of our union, he never held a job down for long. He always believed there was a better and faster way to make money, one with minimum input that would yield maximum output.

He invested heavily in high-risk stocks. He eventually declared bankruptcy because of his bad decisions. After going bankrupt, he wasn't allowed to work in the finance sector and he convinced me to start an advertising company.

As the named owner of the company, my paycheck was used to fund the business, pay our employees, and cover living expenses. To appear rich, he had taken on a lifestyle that was too difficult to maintain.

He told me I would have to stay out of the limelight so he could shine. He would constantly berate me for putting on weight, not looking sexy enough, not dressing rich enough, or looking too ordinary. I even had plastic surgery in the hopes that he would approve of me.

I resorted to lying to get higher-paying jobs because he made me, as his wife, responsible for supporting his business endeavors. Living in constant fear of incurring his wrath on the home front, I worked extra hard to ensure my lies on the professional front were not discovered. Business eventually improved, and we were able to secure a loan from the bank where I worked so we could buy an apartment.

My work ethic was what saved me. My confidence grew as I grew professionally and I began to resist his controlling ways.

Throughout the years, he frequently sought attention from other women; finally it was serious enough for him to want to move on. He began to distance himself from me. He exploited my late nights and long hours at work as the reason for our constant bickering. He said he needed to re-evaluate our marriage. I was in a panicked state and I agreed to allow him to move in with a friend to figure things out.

He needed a way to cash out. He concocted an elaborate plan of how he had opened a trading account in my name that accumulated losses of tens of thousands of dollars.

"How about we sell the apartment, close the business down, get cleared of bankruptcy, start afresh, and live a normal life?" he suggested.

As gullible as it seems now, I jumped at the opportunity to be in his favor again. I sold the apartment and took out extra loans to pay off the debts. As soon as the money came into my account, he emptied every single cent and left me with nothing. Then he held the money as a bargaining chip to negotiate for a quick divorce.

For three days I curled up on my mattress with no food or drink. Drifting in and out of consciousness, I wondered why I had not yet died. As the feeling of being destitute pulled me downward in a spiral of despair, I constantly entertained thoughts of death, yet I did not have the courage to hurt myself. I loathed myself for being weak and stupid. It was no wonder he did not want me. If I didn't die of thirst or starvation, I thought, I should be set on fire and burn to death.

My breakthrough came when I heard a voice in my head: *If you die, he wins! He will be enjoying life with his mistress and living on your hard-earned money.* Sorrow turned to anger, and eventually gave me enough strength to lift myself out of bed.

A sharp pain in my stomach sent me to my knees, and I crawled slowly toward the bathroom. The person staring back in the mirror was unrecognizable; her face pale, with burning eyes. I washed up and hobbled my way to the doctor to get treatment for a urinary tract infection.

The psychological abuse suffered over a decade left a lasting imprint on my psyche and emotional well-being. In the years since, I have had to re-learn how to trust and how to communicate effectively with people. I have again learned to let my walls down to let people in. I have learned how to reframe my mind and to love myself first.

Most importantly, I learned to do the hardest thing of all: forgive myself.

I would be lying if I say the journey to self-love and realization was quick and easy. There still are days when I have doubts. Though I'm not diagnosed with Post Traumatic Stress Disorder (PTSD), I did exhibit symptoms associated with it. Certain triggers will give me flashbacks and feelings of inadequacy. Sometimes, uncontrollable thoughts of the painful aftermath pop into my mind, or I feel unmotivated and detached emotionally.

I still cannot recall the entirety of the fateful three days I spent in bed, but I do remember the key pieces of wisdom I gained through surviving the experience and during my recovery:

Have support and help

No one should ever have to go through tough times alone. Create an internal support system from family and friends, and also consider external support in the form of professional help. A professional counselor will give you an outlet in a safe and non-judgmental environment so you can fully process the myriads of emotions and turmoil within you.

Bring Back 'You'

Allow yourself to receive compliments, solicit them, and ask loved ones to tell you what they love about you. Let yourself make mistakes and accept they're all part and parcel of living. Keep a journal to jot down all the things you enjoyed doing in the past. Bring back the *true* you, reclaim the person you are meant to be. And, as cliché as it sounds, a wonderful way to find yourself is to go on a trip or an adventure.

Stop Self-Sabotaging

Be aware of the pitfalls of getting set in a pattern of self-deprecation. Be kind to yourself. Tune out the little critical voice in your head. Embrace the reality: It is perfectly OK to have doubts! Trust that you can always correct the negative thinking by reframing and reassuring yourself that you're worth it and deserve everything good that is coming your way. Be a constant work in progress as you grow to improve daily.

I can't think of anything more appropriate to end my chapter than sharing with you a Chinese saying: *Zhen Jin Bu Pa Huo Lian, meaning true gold fears no fire.*

Gold can be melted into a molten liquid state under extreme heat; however, its properties remain unaltered and it can be re-designed into anything we desire. Our spirits are like gold. We must first be burned and stripped down, then give rise to something beautiful. Like a phoenix, it's rebirth can only come after burning to ashes.

Biography

Carol Gockel is a transformation coach, speaker, and student of life. Her passion for helping people, particularly women, relearn how to love themselves, grew from her breaking through her own personal adversities. She shares her wealth of experience and knowledge on living and creating a fulfilling life with her clients.

Her personal mission is to inspire and empower people to achieve emotional, spiritual, and financial success.

Carol lives in Singapore with her husband and two children, and she loves to cook and explore the world.

Contact Information:

Connect with Carol on social media:
Instagram: www.instagram.com/carolgockel
Facebook: www.facebook.com/carolgockeltransformation
Website: www.CarolGockel.com
Email: carolgockel@gmail.com

CHAPTER SIXTEEN

All About Action

Arturo Lassiter

Someday

One day

Tomorrow

Later

Four words that prevent us from taking immediate action. How many times have you had a task or goal in front of you and thought about putting it off until someday, one day, tomorrow, or later?

The times in my life when I have taken instant, in-the-moment action on a task, goal, or challenge before me are the times when I have experienced the most progress and success.

I knew from an early age that being an employee and working nine-to-five for forty years was not the plan for my life. Living life according to other people's terms and conditions was not something to which I could conform. I was never the model employee and never would be.

Instead, taking action became the important focus of my life, and it defined the dividing line between two very different outcomes in life.

The expectation of others

As a young man, I dreamed of making it big in the music industry. I had a passion and talent for writing and singing, and I had started a singing group in high school. As a group, we were young, talented, and hungry. Our breakout plan for our future boiled down to attending concerts with the hope of meeting and auditioning for major artists.

In 1994, a popular group called *Immature* had a concert in Kansas City. Being a man of action (even back then), I saw opportunity. Though we had no tickets, we drove an hour to Kansas City with full expectations of meeting the group and seeing the concert. After a couple of failed attempts to go backstage, I spoke with a security guard and learned the name of the hotel where band members were staying.

After we waited for hours, the group finally entered the hotel through the front doors and we began our audition—right there in the lobby. The group's manager said he liked our sound and wanted to fly us to Hollywood, California, to work in the studio. Two weeks later, we received plane tickets to Hollywood.

Since I'd been offered a scholarship to college, I had a decision to make—the biggest decision of my life up to that point. It is not easy to pick up and leave what you've known all your life and move halfway across the country with nothing more than a dream.

How many people would set out for a place they have never been, defying all advice and turning down other "realistic" opportunities, in hopes of creating the life you desperately desired? It is all too easy to let the fear of the unknown paralyze your dreams.

My excitement and deep desire to succeed in the music

business was stronger than my fear, so my brother (my music producer) and I packed up and headed to the Golden State; leaving behind college scholarships, friends, family, and everything familiar. I burned my ships, and there was no turning back. Hollywood presented great opportunities as well as great challenges, and I was prepared to tackle them both.

I eventually signed a deal with Universal Records as a songwriter. This was truly a coup, but I was not satisfied. My dream was to be a vocal artist. Being behind the scenes and writing songs for other artists was great, but it wasn't my dream. I made the best of my situation and did well enough to receive a gold album for songs I had written for a popular R&B group.

My gold album was the key that taught me the magic of residual income or royalties. I learned there was another way to make a living that did not require investing tens of thousands of dollars or sacrificing eight to ten hours a day on the hamster wheel: There was a way to do something *one time*, and get paid for that effort residually.

With jobs, we trade hours of our life for a salary. People say that if you love what you do, you will never work a day in your life. I disagree. Before moving to Hollywood, I worked a few jobs, and all of my employers expected the same from me. I came in when expected, took breaks when expected, stayed when expected, and at the end of two weeks, I was compensated—as expected.

Unfortunately, the amount of compensation was never what *I* expected. Even when I was young I knew if we want more out of life, we must expect more.

We lived in Hollywood for three years, writing and producing for various artists. Besides the gold record, we earned hundreds of thousands of dollars. A couple of twenty-year-old young men with that kind of money in Hollywood, California—can you foresee the problems we ran into? I wish we could have!

While royalties allow you to be paid over and over for the same work, the downside is that if you do not continue to create, the amount of those payments starts to decrease. This happened in our case. As our focus on Hollywood night life increased, our work ethic decreased.

There were friends and family who considered our efforts in the music industry a failure because we did not achieve celebrity status. I feel differently. It is not a failure if you learn the lesson. Hollywood was an opportunity to grow. Hollywood was training ground. Hollywood was a *lot* of experience.

My experience taught me to never get comfortable enough, wherever I was, so I'd lose my fire for whatever got me there.

I also learned to never, ever let anyone's opinion of my dreams become a reality in my mind—especially if they are not living their *own* dream life. Their expectations are just that, theirs.

The chains of the past

After those three years in Hollywood, I returned to Kansas— still not wanting to work for anyone else and still with limited options. For the next few years I worked as an illegal street pharmacist (if you don't mind my using a euphemism).

On December 1, 2004, I had a life-altering experience. I sat in my living room, and for the first time in my life I heard God's voice; there was no way I could misinterpret His words: He told me to *get it together*. Hearing this truly scared me; I like to say it scared me to life, not to death.

That night, I turned everything around.

My girlfriend and I had been living together since I returned from Hollywood, and we had three daughters. Three days later we were solidly married. We started going to church regularly, paying our tithes faithfully, and I served the church with my heart and soul.

After a few months I began to feel stifled, stagnant, and depressed. Although I had made the change to live my life according to God's will, things were still very difficult. It's hard to stay consistent with something you hate doing. I hated working for other people, and nice suits and fresh haircuts do not pay the bills.

I worked a job for a couple of weeks, then I would look at the paycheck I had earned with all my time and effort and never go back. I grew frustrated with myself not being able to provide as I desired.

Fewer than ninety days after my life-altering experience, I learned a very harsh lesson: Bad decisions from the past always have a way of catching up with you.

My wake-up call was being dragged out of my home by police, seeing my wife face down on the kitchen floor in handcuffs and my three daughters at gunpoint as they sat on their beds.

It was a drug raid. The law of reaping and sowing applies to us all. The case was built prior to my salvation, and I was reaping the consequences of my actions. I knew I had let my entire family down.

I sat in the courtroom with my wife and parents in the row behind me and prayed. The Lord answered.

There is man's law and by these laws, I should have spent many years in prison. There is also God's law. I had done a lot of sowing in the community and in our church during the previous ninety days, and while I felt like a failure, God saw my heart. I didn't spend one day in jail. God's law of reaping and sowing prevailed.

I thanked God for my miracle. Safely at home the night of my court appearance, I prayed, "What would you have me to do?"

The next day, I got a call from a local businessman who said he wanted to share something with me over lunch. He introduced me to the idea of network marketing. I had one huge challenge, however—self-doubt. Because of my past, I doubted that people would listen to me or follow me.

In networking, it is important to be able to cast vision and lead, with passion, those with whom you have influence. So, I wrestled with playing full out. I was picking and choosing with whom I'd share my opportunity, avoiding those who I believed were more successful than I was. This was the toughest breakthrough for me.

It took several years, a lot of personal development, and more self-reflection than I had ever done before. Breaking through mental roadblocks created by your past is the toughest, most important, breakthrough to have. It takes a lot of internal evaluation to undress the well-dressed lies you have been telling yourself for years. These are the lies we tell ourselves when we are ready to settle for less than our goal, when we are convincing ourselves the dream is too big, and we begin to negotiate ourselves right off the ledge of our best life.

Fear of the unknown

In 2009, I was introduced to the network marketing company that would change my life. When my wife and I were presented with the opportunity, we did not hesitate. We joined and immediately submerged ourselves into every aspect of personal development. We went to every training event, took notes, listened to every audiotape, and bought every book recommended by the leaders in the industry.

On one Friday evening in 2010, I was up late reading *The Dream Giver*, a book by Bruce Wilkinson. It was a very quick and easy read, an enjoyable story about a visit Mr. Wilkinson made to South Africa, and I was surprised when something happened to me near the end of the book. I was almost finished when I heard the voice of God telling me I should go to South Africa and help free the people financially.

Now, I was thinking the same thing you are probably thinking right now: This is *crazy!*

I had never been to Africa and didn't know a single person anywhere on the continent. I was up the entire night, struggling with the Lord. Around dawn I went to my parents' house for guidance. My vision was so big, I believed they were the only ones who could help me interpret what I was experiencing.

I valued their advice. My father is a bishop and the pastor of our church, and my mother is the co-pastor and a former elementary school principal who was then in the process of starting her own private school.

My wise parents listened to me as I attempted to describe my experience. My eyes were bloodshot from lack of sleep and I was very intense as I told them what I believed God was leading me to do. They advised me to get some rest, pray, and wait for confirmation. After I took a nap, I spent the rest of the day looking at flights to South Africa and trying to make sense of what was happening to me.

On Sunday morning, I woke up for church still in awe of the experience I had the day before. We had a guest speaker, an evangelist from out of state whom I had never met. Toward the end of the sermon, he began to speak to certain individuals, telling them what the Lord was telling him about their situations.

He walked over to me, microphone in hand, and said without preamble or hesitation, "You are called to Africa. I see you in Africa working on some type of business."

I looked over at my father, standing in the pulpit, and he shook his head and took his seat. That was my confirmation.

After the service, my dad told me my aunt worked for the U.S. Embassy and he believed she was stationed in Cape Town, South Africa. It was a sign. When I contacted her and shared my vision, she said only, "When are you coming?"

I had never been to Africa. I felt that four letter word creeping into my spirit. I felt FEAR.

Fear is a very powerful weapon. It is used to control and manipulate people and situations. People use fear to control other people, the enemy uses fear to manipulate our minds. Some fears are rational, and we all have them. Rational fear is our brain's way of keeping us alive. Fear of walking along the ledge of a skyscraper is a rational fear.

However, the worst fears are those internal, irrational fears. People who have an irrational fear of the water will never experience an ocean cruise. People who have an irrational fear of flying may never experience a journey to a different country. Irrational fears keep us from the peak life experiences that make life fulfilling and exciting.

I knew my fear was irrational. Forty-two days later, I boarded the sixteen-hour flight to Cape Town, South Africa.

The moment I touched down in Africa, my fear vanished and I was overcome with excitement and intense purpose. It was a surreal and deeply spiritual moment. I could write an entire book about the forty days I spent in South Africa.

My decision to break through the fear of the unknown, to take that leap of faith, and to follow the dreams that God put in my heart, opened the door for tens of thousands of people to change their lives.

Since then, I have made dozens of trips to eleven different countries, coaching, teaching, training, and empowering people to take their own leap of faith and to follow their dreams.

When God gives you a vision, it is never just for your own benefit. Breaking through those fears was not just for me but for the thousands of people who were waiting to join me on this journey.

My experiences have taught me some very important life lessons.

First, when it comes to business, always look for a way to create residual income. Write a book, score a film, write a song, build a team-building business. A quote by Warren Buffet comes to mind, "If you do not find a way to make money while you sleep, you will work until you die."

I don't want to run a business only to find out it runs me. Even worse, I don't want to sacrifice my dreams by getting hired to build someone else's dreams.

Second, the three ingredients to being successful in life are persistence, perseverance, and posture. You must get after it, stay after it, and do it with confidence.

Lastly, I learned that in everything you do, the key to breaking through is to take immediate action, even when you are gripped by fear. Taking action turns your fears into your fuel.

To God be the glory, and I will see you at the top.

Biography

Arturo Lassiter is a true entrepreneur at heart. As soon as he graduated from high school, he moved to Hollywood, California, where he was a successful singer, songwriter, and vocal producer for Universal Records. He earned a gold album for his songwriting talent.

Lassiter has also proven to be a dynamic leader and trainer in the direct sales industry. From his hometown of Topeka, Kansas, he built an organization of more than ten thousand representatives in twelve countries all over the world by helping others pursue their dreams and goals.

Lassiter earned a bachelor's degree in organizational leadership and transformation change from Friends University. He is a husband, a father, and man of great faith.

Contact Information:

Phone/Text: 785.969.2826
Email: cuatdatopglobal@gmail.com
Social Media: Arturo Lassiter

CHAPTER SEVENTEEN

Work In Progress

Nigel Grant

My father and his younger brother moved to the United Kingdom from Jamaica when they were teenagers, my father first when he was nineteen, and my uncle a few years later when he was just sixteen. Though my mother also was from Jamaica, she was from a different part of the island, and my parents did not meet until they were in the UK. They raised my two younger sisters and me in Wolverhampton, a small city in the West Midlands.

As far back as I can remember, there wasn't a single moment when we were all happy together as a family.

For most of my life, I've worked hard to dredge memories of happiness from my childhood. I remember having fun on a trip to Jamaica with my mother when I was four years old. Being with her, visiting family, and having many "first" experiences which made happy and indelible impressions on my young mind: an airplane ride across the ocean to another country; a ride on a braying donkey; having my hair cut while I was surrounded by people laughing who teased me; and a walk to a local shop, with a relative where I selected red- and white-colored striped mints.

My childhood does have individual moments of relative happiness that I can remember. A few times my father visited me during kindergarten recess as my school was less than a half block away from where he worked, and he would give me candy to share among my school friends.

I remember happy moments when he hoisted me onto his shoulders and we walked down the street and I would accidentally cover his eyes as we walked. I remember hugging him when he came back from a holiday, but that time the happiness was blunted by the fact my parents had separated for the first time.

My parents didn't always get along. I remember when I was still in kindergarten and they must have had an argument. They were in different rooms in opposite ends of the apartment, and I tried a child's version of shuttle diplomacy. I would go to my mother and ask, "Will you be friends with daddy?" Then I would go into the other room and ask, "Daddy, are you going to be friends with Mommy?

After my parents separated for the second time, we lived with my mother, who was very creative with her hands. She would bake cakes with fruit and red wine for special occasions and make smoothies out of beetroot and milk (which sound disgusting but was surprisingly delicious). She crocheted ornamental tablecloths, too; they were starched and ironed so they would curl and be ridged at the edges and ornaments and vases wouldn't easily fall off the table.

There were moments where my sisters, mother, and I would laugh, and there were times when we got told off for being naughty. One of our happiest moments was when my second youngest sister participated in a track event and her team came third. Her trophy was presented to her and the team by an ex-professional football player we all admired.

At fifteen, an event changed the course of my life and

my family's lives. It made the local news just a week before Christmas; the headline read *Blaze Sisters Rescued*.

While we children were asleep, our mother deliberately lit the house on fire and left us in the house. With my neighbors' help, I saved my sisters from burning to death. We suffered smoke inhalation and fortunately none of us were burned.

Mother wasn't sentenced to prison but was sent to a remand center near Manchester for psychiatric evaluation. After the evaluation, she remained in a hospital ward for psychiatric patients for almost a year.

Meanwhile, I lived with my father and my sisters lived with my uncle until we found a house where we all could reside. After my mother's release, my sisters and I were assessed, and we were then allowed to visit her where she lived.

Unfortunately, there was no happily ever after and our family made the local news once more. This time the news headline read *Burned Woman Fights for Life*.

A few days before Christmas, almost exactly a year after the first fire and just a few hours after my sisters and I had visited Mother, she went to the garden behind her house, poured paraffin over herself, and lit herself on fire. She suffered third degree burns over 98 percent of her body, and she soon died in the hospital.

I'm grateful that my sisters had counseling after these horrific actions and events; I know counseling helped them both. I don't remember receiving such assistance. I don't recall wishing I had counseling at that time, but later in life, I realized it would have put me on a better life path sooner.

For at least three or four years, inwardly I was like a zombie, not functioning fully—I was numb. I couldn't feel anything, either positive or negative. I severed all my friendships, I stayed in the apartment where previously my sisters and father had lived, by myself. I was on my own living in a three-bedroom apartment. Since I couldn't work, I survived through social security payments.

All the time, I was planning different ways to commit suicide. One day, someone who lived across the road from where I lived, did do just that, by jumping from the roof of their apartment. After the ambulance and police completed their duties, I watched from my window as council workers hosed the street clean with water. Witnessing the council workers cleaning up the street must have temporarily shocked me enough out of my own suicidal impulses into wanting to find work, but I wasn't really qualified to do anything.

After passing entrance exams, I went to college for a couple of years, a sort of a pre-university education center with work-related courses such as car mechanics. I was functioning by that point, quiet, and I kept my feelings to myself.

I outwardly appeared to be "normal." Inwardly, I was not.

I did start going to church on a regular basis. My father knew of a pastor who had been in my life when I was about six years old, and he reintroduced us. The congregation knew of my story through the news, but never said anything directly to me. It was a place of mental and spiritual refuge.

When I was 25, I moved to London and got a job as a communications operative, which meant I was in a control room answering calls and dealing with incidents. I also decided it was time to wake up and leave the zombie feelings behind, and I started doing crazy adrenalin-fueled things—driving fast cars on a racetrack at Thruxton, skydiving at Headcorn airfield, piloting a plane from Manston airfield over The English Channel and landing at Dunkirk in France, and flying a glider at Dunstable Downs. I wasn't trying to die, I was trying to feel. It worked, and I woke up to new experiences, getting me out of my inner zombie-like state.

My uncle Sam had moved from the U.K. to Canada, and I decided to visit him for three weeks. We had been close when I was growing up, and I appreciated the way he had treated me as an adult rather than as a child. We shared similar interests, and I still remember when he took me to the first museum I ever visited.

We had a good time; I especially enjoyed the time with my aunt, because we shared laughs. While I was in Canada, I made the most of my time and visited places such as Banff, Drumheller, Edmonton, and Calgary.

This was the only time I felt I could enjoy a bit of life. And I still did not think I deserved it.

When I returned, I changed jobs and became a night security guard assigned to various prestigious buildings, one of which included a very active law office where I sat at a reception desk. The solicitors often worked late into the night, and I accepted deliveries of food, legal documents, all kinds of packages. I worked twelve busy hours every night.

I was finally ready to go to university. I studied computing, a demanding subject, during the day, and worked from 8:30 p.m. to 8:30 a.m. in my security guard job—no naps there, and not much sleep at all for the next four years. After work, I took the train from Blackfrairs station to the Elephant and Castle station for the twelve-minute ride to South Bank University, found a quiet corner of the library, and took a two-hour nap. It was even more challenging when one semester I had a 9 a.m. lecture and couldn't nap except for a brief mid-day break. I attended lectures and labs all day.

The next four years were full of intellectual and physical challenges. I didn't think of killing myself during these years. I was mentally awake; though I suffered from constant migraines and physical exhaustion, my mind was clear and alert.

There was a difficult period when I received zero on a pre-exam test. I was devasted. All the hard work, sleepless nights trying to do my job as a security guard and studying during breaks, hadn't worked. For a period of about three to five weeks, I took my notes on that subject everywhere with me. I tried to memorize as much as I could with the time I had. When it came time to do the pre-exam tests, I never got zero again.

When I graduated with a degree in Computing, I finally booked a holiday—my first one in such a long time. I decided to visit Jamaica, where my mother and father had been raised.

I never made it. I went to the hospital instead.

My body had just given out. I had hemiplegia; my left arm and left leg became temporarily paralyzed and just stopped functioning. The hemiplegia was a result of four years of sleep deprivation; it was as though I had been holding on, holding on, and now I no longer needed to do so. Thankfully, it was not permanent paralysis. After a week in the hospital, sensation and movement slowly returned. The only permanent damage was missing my trip to Jamaica. Unfortunately, I still have not made it back to my parents' homeland.

My work career began to look up, though I had to slide in to computer work through the back door. I got into a global industry's computer data center as a security guard, and then wangled my way into being hired as a computer network operative. Later, I was promoted to a network technician and was affectionately known as "router man."

The computer industry had been on a high, however, the

bubble was ready to burst, which no one had expected. This scared me; I was in a good job, one I truly liked, and it was starting to slip away. I did not want to go back to be a security guard, but if I had to, I knew I could.

When the dot com industry's bubble finally burst, it was harsh.

At least I had a fallback career as a security guard. I focused at working my way back into the computer industry, working for a security company that guarded a mining company, and then moving to HSBC bank as a security guard. After less than a year at the bank, I was headhunted to join the access control department. I worked my way up, and now I am within the management structure of HSBC.

When I joined a network marketing company, I saw Johnny Wimbrey on stage. Johnny made me realize that to be successful, you must have self-confidence and the ability to believe in yourself. You must work on yourself mentally to become successful.

I realized I needed to change and develop in a more positive way, so I decided to focus on my personal development. I began by watching YouTube videos—Les Brown, Eric Thomas, the hip-hop preacher, Tony Robbins, Eric Ho, and others. I attended workshops and events that offered a path to the positive change that I was seeking.

Working on myself has been my focus since the epiphany Johnny triggered in me. Though my mental scars are invisible, I'm aware they're still there. Now I am finally breaching the walls of the fortress I built around myself and letting people and experiences inside these walls.

Finally, I've come to terms with what my mother did. After decades, I've been able to forgive her.

It has taken many years to get where I am psychologically; it has not been easy. I have fought the pull of suicide over much of my life. My sisters were burdened by our past, for a while, as they were afraid of passing this burden on to the next generation. They have asked me if suicide was hereditary. I don't know; I do know that the three of us children were terribly scarred by my mother's actions.

I am finally healing.

The changes in me are coming faster now. While I am still a private person, I am making friends and sharing experiences.

These days I do a lot of traveling, and I am finding and enjoying the fun in it, engaging with people of various cultures and costumes, making friendships along the journey. It truly has been amazing. My travels have taken me to Japan twice, New Zealand, Malaysia, Lebanon, America twice, Canada three times, Italy three times, Spain twice, Holland, and Cyprus.

Now I find and appreciate the pleasure in small things. Just yesterday, I moved into a new apartment with windows that frame a beautiful view of trees. I am surprised at the delight I experience as I watch squirrels scurry around the branches, amazingly colored blue jays, and the variety of other birds. I look forward to watching them through the seasons.

My current state has taken decades to achieve. Reflecting on it now, recovering the hard way, with no psychological or counseling assistance, probably was a mistake. I could have reached my sense of wellbeing decades before now.

Enjoy life now while you are able to breathe, regardless of the tragedies that you may have faced. Find a positive way to get through to the other side, whether it is through counseling or other positive methods, because the sooner you deal with the negatives in life, the more you're able to experience the joys of life.

Biography

As a teenage survivor of unspeakable family tragedy, Nigel arrived at his higher education in a roundabout and nontraditional way. While working twelve hours a day and studying full time, he obtained his bachelor's degree in Computing from London South Bank University.

Nigel has found success in the corporate world and is an Incident Support Manager at HSBC Bank in London.

He has a strong interest in world culture and enjoys making new friends as he travels the globe.

Contact Information:

Instagram: sugaman151
Twitter: nigelgranty321
Snapchat: Nigelag1514
Skype: granty1311
Facebook: www.facebook.com/nigel.grant.54
LinkedIn:
https://www.linkedin.com/in/nigel-grant-5b7188a0/

CHAPTER EIGHTEEN

Escape the Ordinary

Nik Halik

As a child, you used to dream. Your mind wasn't shackled by logic, false beliefs, or societal limitations. Everything was possible, and the world was wondrous and magical. Then, as you aged, you started developing false and limiting beliefs about yourself and the world around you. You started buying into societal programming. When people told you something wasn't possible, you believed them. When your peers chose jobs and careers based on their own internal limitations, you followed suit. You started thinking more "responsibly" and "sensibly." And in this process, the flame of your dreams died down to mere embers, and in some cases may have been entirely extinguished.

My invitation to you is to breathe life into your dreams again. Cast off the shackles of your false beliefs and societal programming. Realize the vast majority of your limitations are only in your mind.

What would you do if money was no longer the primary reason for doing or not doing something? What grand adventures would you live? What noble causes would you champion? What great feats would you accomplish?

I was born with a poor biological template. I developed chronic allergies, debilitating asthma, and I was nearsighted. I was medically confined to my bedroom for the first decade of my life. When I was eight years old, a traveling salesman knocked on our front door in Port Melbourne, Australia, and sold my non-English speaking Greek immigrant parents a set of the Encyclopedia Britannica. That set turned out to be one of the greatest influences on my life. It was the spark and secret kindling that set my imagination on fire. My imagination had stretched my mind, and it would never retract to its original dimensions.

I read the encyclopedia constantly and, without my parents knowing, I'd take it to bed with me. I'd shine a flashlight under the sheets, flick the pages of a volume through to a subject that fascinated me, and read until I nodded off to sleep. Sometimes I'd stay awake past midnight, dreaming about the things I was going to pursue in life, and imagining the world that was out there waiting for me.

Growing up, an inspirational character for me was the comic book adventurer named Tintin. Tintin was living the "never grow up" dream, and I traveled the world through his pages, taking in every exotic detail. I read and reread Tintin books in our school library, daydreaming about his magical life. In his various adventures he was a pilot, space explorer, mountain climber, and deep-sea diver. He also climbed the mountains of Nepal, rescued African slaves, battled pirates, and dived down to the deepest abyss of the ocean to explore shipwrecks.

When I reflect on the adventures of Tintin, I realize my

childhood dreams have come true. Many times, in the course of my adventures, I've been in some far-flung destination and had a weird feeling of déjà vu—a Tintin flashback. I was fascinated by space travel. Growing up, I was glued to the TV watching the United States and Russian launches.

Space travel was the big deal then. All this adventure fueled my desire to get in a rocket ship and go myself.

The encyclopedia, the lure of space travel, and the Tintin adventures opened up all the things I wanted to accomplish. I sat down and wrote my highest aspirations in life.

Writing the Script of My Life

I drafted my own screenplay of goals. I was the actor, the producer, and the director. Here I am as an eight-year-old, with my list of ten life goals. Pretty ambitious. Dreaming and thinking big. That list has fueled my life. Since writing down that list at age eight, I've accomplished almost everything on the list. I have two major goals remaining: rocketing to a space station orbiting 250 miles above the Earth and walking on the moon. Even those goals are within my reach.

My Adventures

I became the first flight-qualified, certified civilian astronaut from Australia, and was a backup astronaut for the TMA 13 NASA/Russian space mission. I remain in mission allocation status for a future space flight to the International Space Station.

For a few years, I lived in Moscow and graduated from the Yuri Gagarin Cosmonaut Training Center in Star City. During the Communist era, Soviet cosmonauts were quietly chosen, groomed, and trained behind a veil of secrecy.

My life has been filled with extreme adventures. I have visited over 152 countries. I have trekked with the Tuareg Bedouins across the Sahara Desert. I broke the sound barrier in a modified Russian MIG 25 supersonic interceptor jet traveling at almost Mach 3.2 (2,170 mph, 3,470 kmh) and viewed the curvature of the earth. My rock band performed and toured with big names like Bon Jovi and Deep Purple. I dived down five miles deep in a pressurized biosphere to have lunch on the bow of the shipwreck RMS Titanic in the North Atlantic Ocean.

I have climbed the highest peaks of five continents, including the mighty Mt. Aconcagua in the Andes. I have two more peaks to summit on my attempt to become one of a handful of climbers in history who have climbed the Seven Summits—the highest mountains of all seven of the world's continents. I did a Navy Seals HALO skydive jump with oxygen, above the summit of Mt. Everest in Nepal at over 30,000 feet, on my most recent birthday. I have rappelled into the heart of the most active volcanoes in the world. I have storm-chased tornadoes in the Midwest and hurricanes across the Atlantic Ocean.

I even negotiated with the former deposed dictator of Egypt to spend a night in the nearly 5,000-year-old Cheops Pyramid in Giza, Egypt. I spent the night alone in the King's Chamber of the pyramid and slept in the sarcophagus in total darkness—the very same sarcophagus that Napoleon Bonaparte, Alexander the Great, Herodotus, Sir Isaac Newton, and other giants of history had slept in. Media outlets dubbed me the "Thrillionaire."

"Don't be an extra in your own movie"
—Bob Proctor

My Worldwide Business

During the last two decades, my companies have impacted more than one million people in fifty-seven countries. I deliver keynote speeches and facilitate entrepreneurial training courses around the world. I even get the opportunity to speak in remote locations most foreigners would simply never visit. Just recently, I spoke in the communist "hermit kingdom" of North Korea and taught geography to a classroom of teenagers about to graduate. I have conducted an entrepreneurial mastermind seminar to more than 750 investors and business owners in Tehran, Iran.

Do not go where the path may lead, go instead where there is no path and leave a trail.
—Ralph Waldo Emerson

It's Time to Live Your Dreams

My adventurous life did not happen because I was born into wealth. Lacking a wealthy friend such as Tintin's Captain Haddock, I realized that if I wanted to become an adventurer like Tintin, I would need to develop multiple pillars of income in order to afford such a lifestyle. I wasn't born rich—but I was born rich in human potential. My life by design was never coincidental or lucky. I have merely acted out the script I created for my life—a screenplay I wrote as a young child. My manifested reality was the result of every decision made in my life. I did have medical issues earlier in my childhood, but I refused to be held captive by them. I was forced to clear any obstacles that threatened to obstruct my path of self-discovery.

I'm no more special than anyone else. I've simply set my sights on big goals and have never stopped working to achieve them. There's nothing stopping you from doing the same. You may not care about traveling or anything else I've done. I don't share my life experiences with you because I think you should care about anything I've accomplished, but rather to simply inspire you to live your own version of the ideal life.

There is no shortage of adventures to live and thrills to be experienced. You may want to live on the beach and surf every day. Perhaps you want to go on an epic RV trip. Your dream could be to do frequent humanitarian trips to developing countries. Maybe you just want to spend more time with your family or simply have the leisure time to read more.

Whatever it is for you, go after it. Don't let anyone tell you it's impossible; don't let anything stop you. Life is the greatest show on earth. Ensure you have front-row seats. You have an abundance of opportunities that people in the past could not even have dreamed of. Eliminate all excuses from your mind and vocabulary. Cut off the pessimists and haters in your life. Surround yourself with inspirational people, and immerse yourself in inspirational material. Do whatever it takes to escape the trap of the ordinary. Because I can promise you this:

It is so worth it.

"Start by doing what's necessary; then do what's possible; and suddenly you are doing the impossible"

—St. Francis of Assisi

Biography

Nik Halik, The Thrillionaire® Entrepreneurial Alchemist, Civilian Astronaut, Extreme Adventurer, Keynote Speaker is the founder and chief executive officer of Financial Freedom Institute, Lifestyle Revolution, and 5 Day Weekend®. He became a multimillionaire and amassed great wealth through investments in property, business, and the financial markets. Nik's group of companies have financially educated and life coached more than 1 million clients in 57 countries. Nik generates passive income, building recurring subscription businesses, investing in tech startups, and multi-family apartment complexes. He is currently an angel investor and strategic adviser for several tech start-ups in the United States.

Halik has traveled to more than 150 countries, dived to the wreck of RMS Titanic to have lunch on the bow, been active as a mountaineer on some of the world's highest peaks, performed a high-altitude low-opening (HALO) skydive above the summit of Mt. Everest in the Himalayas, climbed into the crater of an exploding erupting volcano (1,700 degrees F) for an overnight sleepover, and just recently, entered North Korea to expose a sweatshop factory operating illegally for an American conglomerate.

He was the back-up astronaut for the NASA / Russian Soyuz TMA-13 flight to the International Space Station in 2008. He remains in mission allocation status for a future flight to Earth's only manned outpost in orbit—the International Space Station with Russia.

Contact Information:

www.FollowNik.com

CHAPTER NINETEEN

Chasing the Deal

Gerald Walker

All of us dream of that one deal that will change our lives and the lives of everyone we love. The difference between those of us who win our life-changing deal and those who don't is *focus*—the ability to stay focused on our deal even when no one else believes in it or in us.

The deals I have chased are considered unobtainable by most people. My dreams are so big that most people think I'm crazy, but I've always believed I can do almost anything as long as I focus my mind on it.

They're wrong. Deals are always achievable if you have the will, endurance, and the right connection in your life to make them happen.

I have been blessed to travel to twenty-six countries so far in my life and probably have another fifty on my bucket list, and I never really meet strangers. I meet good people in all these countries, and some of them have been instrumental in helping me reach my goal and close huge deals that people with billions of dollars could not close.

My passion is helping people, it's *not* about chasing deals to become rich. When it's all said and done, no one else cares about the cars, the big houses, and the worldly items we accumulate. When our time runs out, all people remember is what we did to help make their lives and other people's lives better.

The older we get, the easier it becomes to realize the final truth:

Life is about leaving a legacy for our family, about getting a deal done that will live long after we are gone.

In my chapter, I hope to share the story of some of my deals I chased and some of the courage it took to close those deals so you can do the same. You can do it, too—if you don't let fear steal your dreams. In *Multiple Streams Of Inspiration Vol. 3*, a book I co-authored, I reminded my readers, "fear is the dream killer for many people."

Yes, I've had many fears in my life. The difference between the average person and me is I choose to face my fear, and I'm willing to absorb the pain that comes with it so I can reach the success I know I deserve.

In September 2004, I traveled to Nigeria to look at opportunities in the security industry there. I had hesitated to visit Africa because of what I had seen on television. If you were going to load a plane with other African Americans and ship us back to Africa, I wasn't about to be on it.

I'm so glad I overcame my fear and went to Africa because I was able to see the opportunities for myself.

Back in Dallas, I had a successful security company, and I believed I was doing very well. My security company was producing revenues of more than $200,000 per month in 2001, but I forgot to remind myself that when you are on top, there is always someone trying to knock you off.

I was selling more than my larger competitors, and they did everything they could to throw a wrench in my smooth-running company. My competitor convinced the company monitoring my contracts to audit every one that had been sent to them. Until the audits were completed seven weeks later, my company could not be funded.

The bogus audit situation was the first real adversity I faced in business, and it caused me to lose hundreds of thousands of dollars. In hindsight, this adversity was the best thing that could have happened because it forced me to look at other opportunities. Without being forced, I would have continued on my nice, profitable, safe path and never looked further.

Something good always comes from something bad. We often can't see it when it's happening and we're suffering but later on, the benefits are clear.

My business setback got me to look at doing business in Africa.

After commissioning a feasibility study on the Nigerian security industry, I knew I needed to make the trip to see the opportunities for myself. When I got off the plane in Lagos, Nigeria, my overwhelming urge was just to book a flight home the next day. I was full of fear and was not accustomed to seeing police carrying AK47s. I knew there were kidnappings and travel could be dangerous in some areas in the country. Lagos was nothing like the cities I visited in the United States and I never felt less at home; it was like New York on steroids. But as soon as I arrived at the hotel, the people were so welcoming and friendly I decided to stay.

Forty-seven days later, I almost cried when I had to leave. There were so many opportunities in Nigeria that I didn't know which one to pursue.

Lagos is the biggest city in Africa, with more than 21 million people. Every business there needed my security service. There were no security cameras in any of the businesses—not even the banks had cameras.

In 2004, the internet was not very prevalent in Nigeria, so I focused on the larger oil companies, which had better internet and wi-fi systems. I pursued Shell Oil, and I designed a camera system to monitor their flow stations—a system no one believed would work. My system was so advanced they sent people abroad to figure out how to duplicate it, but could not.

I chased the deal for at least a year. Shell had multi-million dollar foreign security companies pursuing them, but most of the companies were trying to get the contract without traveling to Nigeria. I had the courage to travel there and show up at Shell's office almost every month for a year until they finally said, "OK, we will give you a project to put cameras on a flow station."

Here is the thing: People saw the glory of my getting the contract, but they have no clue of what I went through to get it, the risky traveling from one Shell Oil facility to another facility doing presentations. I almost died twice in head-on collisions, and those trips were eclipsed by my flight on a small 30-seat plane from Lagos to Shell's Warri facility. That's something I'll never forget.

We were in a terrible storm. When one of the two engines failed, I already had made up my mind that I was about to die on the plane that day. I will never forget it. Everyone was screaming but somehow I was calm. I just held on for dear life and thought, "This is the day I am going to die." I accepted my fate because at least I would die trying to do something to break the cycle of poverty in my family's lives. I had no fear.

Only God could have helped the pilot restart the plane's

engine. I can never forget the little girl crying and embracing her father the whole flight, that image will never leave my mind, or when we landed, how the passengers burst into song because they were so happy to be alive.

When we left the plane and walked into the terminal, we learned that a larger plane that took off minutes after we did crashed during the storm and all 102 passengers had died. It was a surreal moment because that could have been our plane. That's when you ask yourself, "Why am I on the other side of the world chasing this Shell Oil deal?" and "Is it worth it?"

I thought about it, remembering the people who told me I'd never make money in Nigeria or get a contract with Shell Oil. That gave me a renewed spirit to do whatever I had to do to get the contract, even if it meant I would die trying.

You have to believe in something that is worth dying for in order to be successful; I truly know this.

But what matters is that in the end, I beat out all of the big companies. My little tiny company in Dallas, Texas, won a seven-hundred-thousand-dollar solar-powered camera contract from Shell—the first of its kind in Nigeria. I could have given up but quitting is never an option for me, especially when I am focused on a task.

The major companies let fear of traveling to Africa stop them from competing. I had known fear, too, and I'd overcome it.

My next deal was bringing in the first Level Six cash-and-transit armored vehicles (like Brinks armored trucks) to Nigeria. Banks were using pickup trucks escorted by police to move money from bank to bank, and I was told the Central Bank was preparing to make it mandatory for Nigerian banks to start using armored vehicles. It was suggested that because I was in security, I should consider starting a cash-moving business using these armored trucks. I told my source that since it was a cash-intensive business, I didn't think I could afford to do it.

Still, I couldn't get it out of my mind, so I left Nigeria earlier than planned, came back to the U.S. and visited three armored truck builders plus one in Canada. All four companies had a list of African companies trying to buy their trucks and start this type of business in Nigeria. Even the armored truck builders, all multi-million-dollar companies themselves, were trying to export trucks into Nigeria, but none of them could.

The investment would be more than three million dollars to start this type of business in Nigeria. I decided to go for it. One of my Nigerian security company board directors and I talked to officers of a Nigerian bank and flew them to my Dallas offices. Not knowing how the cash-in-transit industry worked, I researched and put together a presentation on how we could start this company in Nigeria. I explained how it would be profitable and protect the banks' cash. They were sold on the idea and the bank funded the entire business startup.

Banks in the United States never would have funded such a startup business. The endeavor to Nigeria changed my entire life.

The next deal I chased was bigger.

I have been to Nigeria seventy-three times and have never been sick thanks to God. Some people are not as fortunate. Nigeria is a place where a hospital won't treat you unless you have money. I have heard many stories of people literally dying in the waiting room. In addition, hospitals are not up to the standards of more developed countries.

My business partner, Atalor Polycarp, is a former banker in Nigeria. He and I decided to take on the challenge of building a state-of-the art thousand-bed hospital that accepts people who can't pay, one that turns away no one in need of emergency medical treatment. Our project is building the largest hospital, not only in Nigeria, but the largest in Africa when it's completed. Our hospital will have the best equipment money can buy.

There is a proven need for a good, modern hospital in Nigeria. Nigerians spend five billion dollars per year leaving their country for medical treatment and checkups.

It has taken five years to plan and get the funding. No one believed we could get the funding to get this project done, and we are now at the finish line for the ground breaking of this project and making this dream a reality. Some people who know that we've been working on the hospital for the past five years are quick to say, "Are you still working on that? It's been five years and nothing has happened."

A major hospital in Dallas just opened a couple of years ago; it took over ten years to get it done. I believe we're right on track.

Here is the thing: When Noah built the Ark, no one believed the rains would come, because God didn't share his vision with them. When you have your vision, you just have to build your dream and wait for the dream to come to fruition, just as Noah had to wait for the rains to arrive.

I am sharing my story to tell you anything—any deal!—is possible when you have a dream. You have to set your goals and pursue your dream and stay focused, doing what it takes to make your dream come true.

My family didn't have money. I come from a tiny town; my graduating class had thirty-two people in it. The only thing our town is famous for is being the place where Bonnie and

Clyde died. I believe it's not about where you came from, it's about the will, determination, and endurance you have. That's what will change the legacy for you and your family.

My father had a third-grade education and my mother a seventh-grade education, but they ran a successful business and reared four kids. I knew from watching them be successful entrepreneurs that one day I had to have my own business, not to become a millionaire or billionaire, but to have the opportunity to help others.

It's not been easy at all; there are so many times I had every reason in the world to quit and just give up. After my sixteen-year-old son committed suicide, I hurt so badly that I really didn't think I could go on. But I *had* to go on, quitting was no option.

Not only does my family depend on me, but so do all the people who work with me. Their hopes and dreams depend upon my dreams coming to fruition; their hopes will be shattered if I quit.

Let me share my vision of what truly drives us to attain our dreams.

Every good, positive deal starts with a dream.

Then we must have hope—hope is the engine of life, and it keeps us and our dreams running every day.

Faith is the key to our engine, and without that key, we can't start our engine of life every day. Every time we insert the key of faith, we must believe our engine will start and we can go anywhere in life we want.

Without dreams, faith, and hope, we are like a car without an engine; we are going nowhere in life.

I hope my chapter will encourage you to chase *your* deals and never give up your dreams. When your life is all said and done, if you have given everything you have, then there will be no regrets, because you will have done all you can do, and all you can do is enough.

I really enjoy speaking wherever I can to spread the word about doing business in Africa; this is my passion. I have a ton of knowledge to share with companies or individuals looking to expand in the African market, and I am going to continue to spread it to help more American companies get into that market.

Biography

Gerald Walker was born to be a successful entrepreneur. After graduating from Grambling State University in 1984, he worked for Frito Lay and Southland Corporation for only seven years before launching his first company in 1992, which became one of the largest African American travel agencies in Dallas, Texas.

In 1995, he transitioned to the security industry, founding his own company a few years later. By the end of his first year in business, his company became the number-one security company in the Dallas Fort-Worth region.

Gerald took on an international challenge in 2004 when he started a security company in Nigeria, and he has experienced many "firsts" there as an African-American entrepreneur. Currently, he is building the largest hospital in Africa and is launching a multi-million-dollar social media platform for global businesses.

Gerald has written two books, *Why African Americans Fear Doing Business in Nigeria* and *Never Make A Permanent Decision Based On A Temporary Situation,* and he has co-authored two more: *Multiple Streams of Inspiration, Volumes 2 and 3.*

Gerald is one the most requested and popular speakers on the complexities and benefits of doing international business in Africa.

Contact Information:

info@geraldwalker.net
Website: www.geraldwalker.net
P.O. Box 1884
Cedar Hill, Texas 75106

CHAPTER TWENTY

From Prison to Purpose

Keenan Williams

We can all agree this is a time of heightened tension between young Black men and women and white police officers throughout the United States. Everyone, from the president to football players, argues about the Black Lives Matter movement, and the subject has become highly politicized.

Twenty-five years ago, though, emotions did not run as high and were not as visible as they are now. At that time, police-criminal relationships in Texas were known to be really bad—maybe even worse than they are now.

I was a drug dealer, a crack addict, and an armed robber who was arrested and jailed forty-six times. *Forty-six*. This was not my plan. It's never anyone's intention to live their life in a way that leads to an arrest record like mine. No third-grader raises his hand and says that he wants to be a drug addict and a habitual criminal. No child wants to spend the rest of their life in and out of prison for the rest of their lives. No parent wants this for their sons or daughters.

Yes, I did the things I was accused of. Yes, I went to prison—angry with myself and frustrated with my life—but not only did I get out, I turned my life around. Nothing would change until I changed my thinking. Now I want to change yours.

I was not a particularly smart or successful armed robber—I robbed drug dealers for a living. I was shot six times. I was addicted to crack cocaine for seven years. I was homeless for four years. Somehow, I survived.

I was headed to prison for a long time and I was not exactly the kind of young man who was normally treated with respect by the infamous Texas police.

Then a white cop treated me with respect and changed my perspective.

How did all this happen?

Being a criminal was not my preordained fate. I grew up in Grand Prairie, Texas. Growing up, I was always aggressive in my behavior; I fought a lot and protected my two younger brothers and cousins. My dad told me I could never lose a fight; if I did, I couldn't come home until I won.

When I was nine years old, I had a fight with two brothers who were my neighbors and I beat them up. They went to get their cousins to fight me. My dad gave me a 44-magnum and told me to sit on the stairs with the gun.

"When they come up the stairs, *shoot* them," my dad instructed. Of course, I needed to do whatever my father said, because I was afraid of him.

I sat there all day, and by God's grace, they did not come home.

I lived in a dysfunctional household. My dad had an anger problem and he used to fight with my mom all the time, so I grew up with violence in the house. My mother, brothers, and I were cowed by my father.

I loved school because school gave me the opportunity to have friends and play football. Being a sophomore and playing on the varsity football team was a real thrill. Football also gave me the opportunity to be aggressive and release my anger in a healthy way.

Going into my senior year, all the major colleges were interested in me for a scholarship. They wrote me letters and visited me; I kept them away from my family because I was embarrassed by the dysfunction.

Then I was injured in the very first game of the year. My life, my prospects, my entire worldview changed in an instant. My football career was over before it could even start.

The day I came home from the hospital after the surgeons told me I'd never play football again, I found out my parents were divorcing. That was the blow that crushed my hopes. Home didn't feel like home anymore. I dropped out of school because I had no direction, correction, or dreams.

I turned to the Navy to see if I could find a new life there, but the screws in my knees meant I couldn't find a career in service. I was out of options. I did the only thing I could think of. I quit high school two weeks before graduation and took to the streets.

I joined a gang because it gave me a false feeling of family, an emotion I needed, and started selling and using drugs. By the time I was 19, I was addicted to crack cocaine, living in abandoned houses with no lights, power, or running water, and turning to the Salvation Army for assistance. Becoming desperate, I began robbing drug dealers to support my habit and went on a spree of committing aggravated robberies against them. For the next several years, I was in and out of jail 45 times, shot six times, stabbed, beaten with a bat, and left in a ditch to die. I survived two hits that were put out on me.

By my mid-20s—a time when a young man is supposed to be settling himself in his career and life, maybe even starting a family—I was living on rock bottom.

The forty-sixth time I was arrested, I received my lucky break. Detective Alan Patton of the Grand Prairie Police Department was my arresting officer. I knew I was going away for a long time, and I was frantic. I needed to say goodbye to my children, grandmother, brothers, and mother, and I asked for twenty-four hours.

Detective Patton believed in me. I have no idea why he saw something worthwhile in the habitual criminal talking to him, but he did. He knew I was putting myself in danger, and this type of living never ended well, for me or the people who loved me. He was the first person in years who showed me respect, the respect that I stopped showing myself ages ago. He treated me like a fellow human being.

"Yes, Keenan," he told me. "I trust you to turn yourself in. You can have twenty-four hours to see your family." He even instructed the other police officers to stay out of my way during that time.

During those 24 hours, I visited my family and reflected on my life up until that point. Then I turned myself in, right on time. Detective Patton showed me respect and I did the same for him in return because he went out on a limb for me.

I was tried for a variety of crimes, ranging from aggravated robbery and assault to terroristic threats and drug charges, and found guilty of charges of aggravated robbery, unlawfully carrying a weapon, assault, terroristic threats, forgery, and unauthorized use of a motor vehicle. I spent six years in a Texas prison. It wasn't easy time.

To say that the first four years of prison were hard would be an understatement. I was still angry at the world. Bitter about my injury. Upset with myself about the choices I had made, but I felt like it was everyone else's fault that I was in prison and had been on drugs. I still hadn't taken responsibility for my choices, decisions, and actions at that point. I felt like I was already on this path and there was no getting off it, so I plowed forward. Those first four years, I fought being incarcerated and I fought everyone else.

I saw ministries, including Mike Barber Ministries, come to prison and speak with inmates. Every time they came, they were very nice and kept telling me about this wonderful God and that He loved me. Because I had taken on the Muslim faith, it made it even harder for me to hear that a Christian "God" could love me.

One day, I was in solitary lockup for fighting, and I said to God, "If this Jesus that everybody keeps talking about is the way to go, I'll be okay with that if He could change my life." That night, I was overwhelmed by a presence I had never felt before.

I knew I wanted to be my best self not only in prison, but after my release. I didn't want to go back to the person I was before. I wanted to move forward, and I started making use of my jail time in many positive ways. I focused solely on becoming mentally, physically, and (above all) spiritually strong. Those three aspects of my life would make me unstoppable.

There are two good things about prison; they let you have books and they have educational programs. I took advantage of both. For the last two years of my incarceration, I devoted myself to self-education, reading more than two hundred books on the topics of etiquette, integrity, parenting, ethics, business, and career success. I read the Bible every day.

In my reading, I discovered a quote from Abraham Lincoln that changed my life: *If I had forty-five minutes to chop down a tree, I would spend the first thirty minutes sharpening my axe.* I applied that quote to everything I did, in every area of my life, for the next two years and every day since. My time in prison taught me about stamina and persistence. Once I started, I never gave up. I knew I had options. It was time for me to take control of my life.

I also began studying for my college degree in air conditioning and refrigeration. I realized at that point that education would become the key to my success. Earlier, in high school, I had taken so much for granted, and I didn't apply my mind, relying instead on football. Back then, the only thing that limited me was my thinking. My thinking was focused on what I saw as my limitations.

Now I know that it doesn't matter who my parents were, where I was born, or what color I was. Education created more opportunities and produced more choices and decisions that became the formula for my success.

While I was in prison, I began to plan my success. I learned to walk and speak differently. I practiced gestures that would not offend people when I was speaking to them. When I sat down to eat, I made sure my posture was correct and took my time eating. In my mind, I was preparing to sit at the table with dignitaries.

Preparation became the focal point in all my daily activities. I began to understand the significance and the importance of my time in prison, and I learned that time was the only thing in life that I could not get back, therefore it became my greatest treasure.

My days in prison were planned from the time I woke

up until the time I went to bed. I had a schedule. I ran five miles every other day because I knew I would not have any transportation when I got out. I studied and excelled in the game of chess because I likened it unto life. My dream became a desire to go from "prison to the White House."

When I got out after serving my full six-year sentence, I looked up the police officer who changed my life. I met with Detective Patton to shake his hand and thank him.

"You changed my life," I told him, and I was surprised at how moved he was. He later told me that my actions changed his life as well.

In a public meeting where we shared the podium years later, he told the audience, "My career was a success because I had something to do with this man making a change in the way he lived life."

By then he had retired as chief of detectives. I was surprised when he told other police officers, "Keenan is the poster-adult for what can happen if you just show a little mercy and grace to the person who's going to go to jail." He told them he was proud of me.

My stamina, persistence, and focus gave me the chance to start again. People began to take notice of my story. I began speaking at schools, stressing how important education is in young lives. I wanted children to use my failures and success as lessons—they didn't have to learn the hard way, like I did.

I began speaking with groups of police officers about the importance and impact of what Officer Patton did for me. The way he treated me was the first step in my journey. I cannot thank him enough for what he did for me and my family.

Now I'm a successful businessman and entrepreneur, a finance director who has relationships with more than 40 banks with whom I partner. I am a happy father, and a motivational speaker at prisons, schools, businesses, and police departments, and a life coach.

I'm a re-entry activist. I tell my story at churches and businesses, stressing my message of encouragement, stamina, persistence, and education. I want people to change the way they think about others and themselves. My time in prison led to my new faith and new philosophy—my belief that *anyone* can be transformed by the renewing of their mind.

As the chairman of the Minority Engagement Committee for the Dallas County Republican Party, I help educate minority communities and leaders about the true platform of the Republican Party and its successes. I have also spoken to the top people at the Texas Department of Corrections about reducing recidivism.

I have met President Trump and Vice President Pence and have shared the stage with congressmen, state representatives, senators, and educators. I visited Barack Obama in the White House and attended his inauguration and his inaugural ball.

I'm involved in politics to help bring a balance to this country, and to change and amend laws to help those who are living unfortunate lives. There are people who just can't imagine the life I had to live, the life other people are living in America. I've seen things many of our elected officials have never seen, and experienced pain they will never experience.

I was born for a time such as this and my life has prepared me to be a part of history in the making. When preparation meets opportunity, it becomes the formula for success.

In America, people do not fail because of a lack of opportunity. They fail because they're not prepared when opportunity presents itself.

It doesn't matter who you are and what you've done; you can *still change*. I want my story to give hope to the people who are on the corners, in the drug houses, in the prisons and in the jails. I also want to give hope to our elected and appointed officials; we all need to know that together we can make a difference and make America the greatest place on earth.

"Attitude plus aptitude creates the altitude of your dream"—the A-plus factor!

Biography

In 1985, Keenan Williams was a high school senior and football star in his hometown of Grand Prairie, Texas, with a promising future in football until a serious injury derailed those hopes. At the time, his parents were divorcing, which further added to his anguish. Feeling he had nowhere else to go, he took to the streets.

By the time he was 20, he was addicted to cocaine, living in abandoned houses with no lights, power, or running water, and turning to the Salvation Army for periodic assistance. Williams soon began robbing drug dealers to support his habit and went on a spree of committing aggravated robberies against them. For the next several years, he was in and out of jail thirty times, shot six times, stabbed, beaten with a bat, and left in a ditch to die.

At age 25, he was sentenced to prison for six years for a multitude of crimes ranging from aggravated robbery and assault to terroristic threats and drug charges.

Fifteen years later, Keenan is an entrepreneur and well-respected motivational speaker, sharing his inspirational story on both national and local television and radio and bringing encouragement to those who have lost hope.

Contact Information:

Email: Keenan@KeenanWilliams.net
Facebook: Keenan Williams Motivational Speaker.
LinkedIn: Keenan L. Williams
Website: KeenanWilliams.net

CHAPTER TWENTY-ONE

Give Back and Inspire!

Kimber Acosta

I held your hand and told you I loved you. You looked deeply into my eyes. Then your eyes closed for what seemed like an eternity (but was only a moment). You swallowed and nodded your head.

Then you opened your eyes and took your last breath.

At that moment, it all came back to me: my biggest fear as a child was that I would lose you. Today, that fear became reality.

For nearly thirty days and nights, I kept vigil by your side. I watched your monitors, asked hospital staff questions, and listened to beeps and compression sounds from the machines attached to your fragile body. Through every crisis, you fought for your life on the inside—and I fought for your life on the outside, questioning every action the hospital staff took.

My mother had been my world since forever. I looked up to her, respected her, loved her, and cherished her. Whenever she went out, I cried for her and anxiously awaited the hugs and kisses I would receive when she returned. She was my world. All I ever wanted to do was make her proud of me. All I ever wanted was to be just like her.

Then one day my whole world came crashing down. I was 10 years old. I did not quite understand what was happening or why. All I knew was I felt as if my life was ending and I could not breathe.

My mother left me.

I remember vividly her telling me to keep her stuffed Pink Panther and to take care of him until she returned for me. She promised she would come back for me someday and I could give him back to her then. I cried and held on tight to Pink Panther. I slept every night with him. I took care of him. I protected him. All so my mother would be proud of me the day she came back. Days turned into weeks, weeks turned into months, and months turned into years. It seemed as if she was right there in front of me, just an arm's length away, living her life, but I could not reach her or be a part of her world.

Did you ever look at the horizon as a child and think, "If I just keep walking, one day I will be able to touch the sky?" That is how I felt knowing Mother lived so close, yet so far. I would see her. I would run up and hug her. I would beg her to let me come home.

The year was 1984, I was 12 years old. I was losing all hope. The pain inside me was growing beyond my ability to handle it. I wanted to die but at the same time, I wanted to live.

Two years had passed since my mother left and it was just over a year since my dad had been given a choice—his children or his new family over his children. I wanted so much to be back home with mother. I would see her. I would beg her to just let me come home. There was no room in her new life for me. I cried almost every night.

Every day I dragged myself out of bed and forced myself to go on with the day and do my school work. There was no foster system to be trapped in. My second oldest sister and I were two of the few who fell through the cracks. If not for a few families who took us in, I am not sure where we would have ended up.

I was a little girl who had to grow up fast and figure out how to survive and pay her own way in a world about which she knew nothing. I picked rocks out of fields for a local farmer. I detasseled corn, delivered newspapers, cleaned dog kennels, bussed tables at a restaurant, worked in a plastic factory, and whatever else I could throughout those years to make money to survive.

My own determination—my own will to survive—kept me in school. Just when I wanted to give up and lost all hope, in 1984 I was given something to help me hold on. That was the year that the The Cosby Show first aired and the show changed my life. It kept me alive. I am not sure if I would be here today if it was not for that show—especially Phylicia Rashad, who played Clair Huxtable, the mom on the show. It was through her character's love for her children that I found a way to survive some of the toughest years of my life.

When I was facing a tough week, I would just tell myself, "It will be okay if I can just hold out until Thursday and see Clair." To see Clair hug her children, give them advice, show them love, and discipline them when they did wrong was touching. When she did those things for them, it was like she was doing that for me. I would sit back and pretend I was one of the Huxtable children and Clair was my mother. I took in her advice, hugs, lectures, and love. Whenever I was at my lowest, thoughts of her being the mother she was on that show saved me.

I remember crying—with a blade in my hand, just wanting the pain of my life to stop. I wanted to erase the years of loneliness and would start thinking that a swipe of that blade would take it all away. But then Clair would pop into my head and I somehow could feel her hugs and heard her saying, "Everything is going to be all right, just have faith."

I would tell myself I just need to hold out until Thursday night when *The Cosby Show* was broadcasted and everything would be all right. I would then put the blade down, take some deep breaths, close my eyes, and pray I could make it another day. Feeling love from a fictitious TV character helped me find my way.

And look, I am here today.

Throughout those tough years, Clair saved my life many times. With pills, blade, or gun in my hands, it was Clair's love for her children that made me put them down. Clair showed me the person and mother I wanted to be. Now all these years later and having raised two amazing sons, I look back and thank God for bringing Clair into my life.

When I was in high school I wrote a letter to Rashad and shared with her some details of my life and told her how her character on *The Cosby Show* saved me. I thanked her for coming into my life and helping me keep my faith at a time when I felt all was lost. About a year later, I received in the mail, a picture of Rashad. On it was written, "Thank you for your nice letter, all the best, Phylicia Rashad."

Her response—her taking the time to respond to my letter—meant a lot to me. To this day, that picture hangs on a wall in my home. Each day before I leave home, I look at Phylicia, smile, and give thanks to Clair, my TV mom, for shining the light down my dark and lonely path I was on.

As my children were growing up, reruns of *The Cosby Show* were on TV. It warmed my heart that I was able to sit and watch the show with them. I told them that if it had not been for Clair, none of us would have been there and how she helped me hold onto my faith at a time when I had none.

Now, I am sure you are wondering where is the Pink Panther? Well, he is right here on my desk above my computer. Taking a break from typing, I looked up into his eyes. He has been with me through the ups and downs, the laughter and tears, the joys and sorrows, and the faith and fear.

So many people gave up on me and said I would never amount to anything. For the life I lived, they said I should have ended up either dead, in jail, an alcoholic, or drug addict.

Despite their lack of faith and because of Clair, I persevered. I got out of that town. Through the grace of God, my list of accolades is long and continues to grow. I took my struggles and used each one to champion others.

My career chose me. It was not what I was studying in college. As a child, I dreamed of being a country singer or an officer for Interpol, but God had other plans for me. Through His guidance, I became a journalist and photographer. My career has evolved into hosting my own show online since 2008 and anchoring a news show since 2009. From there, my career has continued to evolve into producing and directing shows for online and cable.

My career has taken me to all corners of the United States to cover and share stories on youth, elders, business people, tribes, artists, and our environment.

Who would have ever thought some little 10-year-old girl whose mother and father abandoned her would:

- Host the Native American Music Awards red-carpet event live online in front of millions of viewers around the world.
- Be the only photographer physically on the red carpet at the Grammy Awards.

- Follow and photograph Tiger Woods and Notah Begay III all weekend during The Presidents Cup.
- Be on the track of the Indy 500 taking photographs.
- Take a private personal tour with Loretta Lynn before the opening of her museum.
- Be one of two photographers in the pit of Tina Turner's opening night of her 24/7 world tour.
- Be one of only a handful of media to cover "Building Bridges: Religious Leaders in Conversation with the Dalai Lama."
- Have her photographs and writing featured and published online, and in magazines, newspapers, books, tour booklets, newsletters, brochures, music videos, and albums all around the world.
- Have pieces of her work hung in museums across the country and issued as limited-edition prints.

Who would have thought that the same little girl who never finished college would one day get to be the commencement speaker for graduates at a college, sharing her story of triumph?

Me neither, but look at me now.

I have never resented my parents for the choices they made because I would not be who I am today if I did not go through every struggle I faced and learned every lesson life offered. I would not have been able to meet the people I have met or share their stories for others to witness their strengths. All I ever wanted was to make my mother and father proud.

One day in 2015, my phone rang and my oldest sister broke the news that she had stage four triple-negative metastatic breast cancer. Six months later, my mother had a massive stroke leaving her paralyzed on her left side.

Within a year, I sent my youngest son off to the military,

and watched my sister wither away and my mother give up. Through that period, with the help of my oldest son, I put my career on hold and spent many hours weekly on the road to be with my sister and mother.

Every week I would give my mother a hug and as I turned to leave she would cry and beg me to take her with me.

The tables had turned.

Instead of a little 10-year-old girl crying for her mother to take her home, the mother was crying and begging to be brought home. I would have given anything to bring her home. The pain of leaving each week tore me apart.

I wondered if what I felt was the pain she experienced every time I cried for her all those years ago. I never knew the reasons behind what she did or the choices she made. She took the answers with her when she died.

But I had a tough choice myself. My sister never told our mother she was dying and she swore me to secrecy. She did not want to worry our mother; she wanted our mother to focus on getting better.

I had to choose: Do I take our mother to my home more than four hours away or keep her down by the family so that I could also be there for my sister during her last days? Mother did not understand, but how could she? She had no idea her oldest child was dying.

My sister died October 27, 2016. Five months later, on March 19, 2017, my mother took her last breath as I held her hand.

You never realize how close death is until you see someone you love take their last breath.

If a 10-year-old girl can grow up and turn her struggles into triumphs and make a difference for others, so can you. Being homeless was never my biggest fear. My biggest fear was losing my mother. I faced that fear twice. I survived her leaving when I was a child and look at all I have done since. I survived her death as well, though it was just as painful as when she left me behind as a little girl.

I will continue to turn my pains into strength to give back, to rise, inspire, and be my brother's keeper, as we all should be.

Biography

As a producer, director, news anchor, entertainment host, editor, marketing/advertising director, journalist, photographer, solutions authority, and online guru, Kimber Acosta has been setting trends while expanding her career titles and gaining accolades for three decades.

Her career path was set at age 19 after getting stuck in a snowstorm more than four hours from her hometown. After she ran out of money to survive the winter in an unfamiliar town where she lived out of her car and slept on the couches of new friends, she stumbled upon a job opening in the mailroom of a national newspaper with worldwide distribution.

Acosta was hired despite not knowing anything about computers or writing. Whenever she wanted to do something to advance her career, her editor told her "to figure it out." Kimber took that as a sign to follow through with whatever she thought was necessary to succeed.

Through her own determination and compassion for others she has built a self-taught career on lifting others up by continuing to shine a light on those that she felt had been left in the dark.

Kimber brings a multicultural approach to her unique worldview; her ethnic background is a mixture of Turtle Mountain Ojibwe, Canadian Cree, French, and German. She lives in northwest Wisconsin and has two children, Animikii and Miskwagiizhig, whose names mean Thunderbird and Red Sky in Ojibwe.

Contact Information:

Email:
giizhig@gmail.com

Websites:
https://www.KimberAcosta.net
https://www.SynergyAllianceSociety.com
https://Kimber12.WorldVentures.biz

Social Media:
https://www.facebook.com/KimberlieAcosta
https://www.linkedin.com/in/kimberacosta
https://www.instagram.com/dare.to.live.freedom.fighter
https://twitter.com/Kimber_Acosta
https://www.youtube.com/giizhig

CHAPTER TWENTY-TWO

The "Real" You

Les Brown

Sometimes it's not about changing to become the person you *want* to be; it's about changing to become the person you *need* to be. There is a whole big, expectant world out there waiting on you to do the things you were destined to do – and the only obstacle in the way is YOU. Personal growth can help you conquer that obstacle, but you must first be a willing participant.

Once you have decided that you are that willing participant, follow these four easy stages of increased awareness to help you begin this journey to a "new you." Let's take a quick look at how 1) self-knowledge, 2) self-approval, 3) self-commitment and 4) self-fulfillment intertwine to help you consciously step into greatness.

First of all, in order to see yourself beyond your current circumstances, you must master **self-knowledge**. Simply ask yourself, "What drives me?" And then pause long enough to hear your response. Try to understand what outside forces – positive or negative – are influencing your answer. Many of us suffer from what I call "unconscious incompetence." That means we don't know that we don't know, which leaves the door wide open for others to tell us what we think we need to know. Therefore, before you can fully wake up and change your life, you must understand the frame of reference from which you view the world. Study

241

yourself, study the forces behind your personal history, and study the people in your life. This will help liberate you to grow beyond your imagination.

The second, and perhaps most crucial, stage of personal growth is **self-approval**. Once you begin to know and understand yourself more completely, then you must accept and love yourself. Self-hatred, self-loathing, guilt and long-standing anger only work to block your growth. Don't direct your energy toward this type of self-destruction. Instead, practice self-love and forgiveness and watch how they carry over into your relationships, your work and the world around you, opening up the possibility for others to love you, too. If you need help in boosting your self-approval, try these steps: 1) focus on your gifts, 2) write down at least five things you like about yourself, 3) think about the people who make you feel special, and 4) recall your moments of triumph.

When you are committed to taking life on, life opens up for you. Only then do you become aware of things that you were not aware of before. That is the essence of **self-commitment**. It's like the expanded consciousness that comes whenever I commit to a diet. Suddenly, everywhere I turn, there is FOOD! Or how about when you buy a new car? Suddenly you notice cars exactly like yours, everywhere you go. Well, likewise, when you make a commitment – when your life awareness is expanded – opportunities previously unseen begin to appear, bringing you to a higher level. In this posture, you are running your life, rather than running *from* life.

The fourth stage of self awareness is **self-fulfillment**. Once you have committed to something and achieved it, you then experience a sense of success and empowerment, otherwise known as fulfillment. Your drive for self-fulfillment should be an unending quest; a continual sequence of testing self-knowledge, fortifying self-approval, renewing self-commitment and striving for new levels of self-fulfillment. Once you have accomplished a goal and reached a level of self-fulfillment, it is then time to go back to the first stage in the cycle.

These four stages create synergy for a conscious awareness of your personal growth. But what about learning to deal with all this from a subconscious standpoint? A very interesting book I have read entitled, "A Whole New Mind," by Daniel H. Pink, explains that the key to success today is in the hands of the individual with a whole different kind of thinking than what our informational age has molded us to. The metaphorically "left brain" capacities that fueled that Information Era, are no longer sufficient. Instead, ""right brain" traits of inventiveness, empathy, joyfulness and meaning – increasingly will determine who flourishes and who flounders." (Pink, 2007)

I highly recommend that, in the midst of your busy schedule, if you haven't done so already, pick up this book and engage yourself to a fresh look at what it takes to excel. As I mentioned before, the only real obstacle in your path to personal growth and a fulfilling life is you. If everything around you is changing and growing – then change and grow. Do it today. Remember, we are all counting on you to step into your greatness!

Now even after making all of these changes what would you say if someone walked up to you and asked, "Who are you?" Would you stutter or hesitate before giving some sort of answer? Would you make up something that sounded impressive, but that you know isn't exactly true? Well, to accurately answer the question of who you are, you must first get in touch with the person who lives and breathes on the inside of you.

When you know and understand who you were made to be, you can begin to tap into the innate power of your own uniqueness. That power allows you the freedom to no longer let life hold you back because of nonsense based on what you've done or not done. It gives you the positive energy to move forward in spite of those things.

You are a unique individual. Think about it, out of 400,000,000 sperm, one was spared to allow you to be here today. Then once you got here, you came with total exclusivity! I know for a fact, as a twin myself, how you can look like someone else, even sound like that person, yet when you consider the total you, there is only one. Wow! Just let that thought sink down in you for a moment.

Now, hopefully that helps you to realize that there is a certain quality on the inside of you that was given to you – and only you – in order to make a difference in this world. Whatever that quality is, it was not intended for you to sit on it, or waste it away. Oh no, it was given to you for a purpose! You cannot, however, learn what that purpose is unless you look inside and see what makes your existence so special.

Don't waste time trying to find "you" in other people. When you compare yourself to others, or try to be like them, you deny yourself – and the universe – the opportunity to be blessed by the gifts and talents that were given only to you. You are destined to achieve great things in *your* own special way; not in the same manner as your friends, relatives, co-workers, colleagues or even mentors. Doing so will only leave you unsatisfied. When you are not satisfied, regret creeps in.

If you don't know this already, let me share a little secret with you: In order to live a good life – a life full of purpose and resolve – you must live it with NO REGRETS!

Most people go through their whole life with a long "would've, could've, should've" list. The truth of the matter is, once you've lived through a day, an hour, or a minute, it's done. You cannot go back. So get over it! Go forward! There's so much more for you to accomplish that you don't have time to live in the past trying to fix things.

Keep in mind, though, that living in the past and reflecting on the past are two totally different things. You *can* look back –

and you should – in order to determine what it was about certain experiences that brought you joy and satisfaction, or grief and despair; what caused you to grow and expand your horizons, or left you stagnant and short-sighted.

Although you cannot relive the past, you can learn much about yourself as a result of having lived it. That requires a lot of honesty with yourself, as well as a willingness to do **whatever it takes** to reach your destiny. Of all the things you can acquire in this life, the most valuable has to be the knowledge of what role you are to play on this earth, for the sake of your destiny.

My favorite book says to *"Lean not on your own understanding, but in all your ways, acknowledge Him and He will direct your paths."* In other words, don't rely solely on your own insight regarding what your role is. There's a Creator who made you and knows you better than you know yourself. Therefore, in everything you do, in every direction you take, recognize and consult with that Creator. That's what it means to look on the inside – not at others.

Now, you will have a real answer when someone asks, "Who are you?" You can assure them that, without a shadow of a doubt, you are not here by accident. You can articulate with unwavering conviction what it is you were put on this earth to do. **Learn to do this and watch the real "you" shine through!**

Biography

Les Brown is a top Motivational Speaker, Speech Coach, and Best-Selling Author, loving father and grandfather, whose passion is empowering youth and helping them have a larger vision for their lives.

Les Brown's straight-from-the-heart, high-energy, passionate message motivates and engages all audiences to step into their greatness, providing them with the motivation to take the next step toward living their dream. Les Brown's charisma, warmth and sense of humor have impacted many lives.

Les Brown's life itself is a true testament to the power of positive thinking and the infinite human potential. Leslie C. Brown was born on February 17, 1945, in an abandoned building on a floor in Liberty City, a low-income section of Miami, Florida, and adopted at six weeks of age by Mrs. Mamie Brown, a 38 year old single woman, cafeteria cook and domestic worker, who had very little education or financial means, but a very big heart and the desire to care for Les Brown and his twin brother, Wesley Brown. Les Brown calls himself "Mrs. Mamie Brown's Baby Boy" and claims "All that I am and all that I ever hoped to be, I owe to my mother".

Les Brown's determination and persistence searching for ways to help Mamie Brown overcome poverty and his philosophy "do whatever it takes to achieve success" led him to become a distinguished authority on harnessing human potential and success. Les Brown's passion to learn and his hunger to realize greatness in himself and others helped him to achieve greatness in spite of not having formal education or training beyond high school.

"My mission is to get a message out that will help people become uncomfortable with their mediocrity. A lot of people are content with their discontent. I want to be the catalyst that enables them to see themselves having more and achieving more."

Les moved to Detroit and rented an office with an attorney, where he slept on the floor and welcomed his reality stating that he did not even want a blanket or pallet on the cold, hard floor to keep him motivated to strive. In 1986, Les entered the public speaking arena on a full-time basis and formed his own company, Les Brown Enterprises, Inc..

Les Brown rose from a hip-talking morning DJ to broadcast manager; from community activist to community leader; from political commentator to three-term State legislator in Ohio; and from a banquet and nightclub emcee to premier Keynote Speaker for audiences as big as 80,000 people, including Fortune 500 companies and organizations all over the world.

As a caring and dedicated Speech Coach, Les Brown has coached and trained numerous successful young speakers all over the nation.

Les Brown is also the author of the highly acclaimed and successful books, "Live Your Dreams" and "It's Not Over Until You Win", and former host of The Les Brown Show, a nationally syndicated daily television talk show which focused on solutions and not on problems.

Contact Information:

www.lesbrown.com

 thelesbrown

 @LesBrown77

 @thelesbrown

 LesBrown

 LinkedIn@

CHAPTER TWENTY-THREE

One Day
Can Change Your Life

Jonathan Long

One day changed my entire life.

I remember it like it was yesterday: April 5, 2010. It was a day of excitement—both the Opening Day for Major League Baseball and the NCAA National Championship basketball game.

I was eager to go to my first baseball Opening Day event. My friends and I began tailgating around 11 a.m. at the Coors Light Tailgate Party Tent. I was overjoyed because of the pleasant time I was having with the people closest to me.

The atmosphere was like none other I had felt up until that point in my life. Live music blasting, ice cold beer, bright sunshine beaming down on us. Not too hot, not too cold, just right. We continued our tailgating up until the game started and then chugged our drinks so we could head inside for the opening pitch.

We walked into Globe Life Park, and as soon as we stepped in, you could feel an atmosphere of excitement. Lots of smiles, lots of laughter, and great vibes all around me. The

Texas Rangers were opening their season against the Toronto Blue Jays. We went back and forth between our seats to watch the game, the bar for drinks, and the food shops. (I just had to get myself one of those delicious turkey legs.) It took me three innings of searching to find the right spot, but I finally found it.

As I approached the counter to order, my salivary glands were watering just thinking about how good this was going to be. After I was served my order, I immediately bit into my turkey leg and it was like an explosion of indescribably amazing flavor in my mouth. It was well worth the wait. After eating, we went back to one of the bars in the ballpark for another round of drinks, then we went back to our seats and finished watching the game.

It was a close game. After the seventh inning, the score was tied 3-3. In the eighth inning, the Blue Jays pulled ahead by one. Heading into the ninth inning, everyone in the ballpark was on edge. The Jays did not score in their half of the inning, and now it was our turn. After just a few at bats, we scored the tying run. Then just a few batting attempts later, we scored on a walk-off run to win the game with a final score of 5-4.

It was a wonderful day: The Rangers came back and won and I was feeling good from the positive vibes in the stadium. The drinks helped, and my stomach was full of food, and the day was not over yet.

After the game, I found myself with my friends at a local bar, watching the NCAA Championship game, Duke vs Butler. It was a nail-biter that came down to the last shot. Duke was up 61-59 with just two seconds left. Butler inbounded the ball to half court to Gordon Haywood, who turned and put up the shot from around the half-court line. It seemed like the ball was in the air for an eternity as it traveled to the basket. It almost seemed like it was going to go in the basket. The ball hit the inside of the rim and rattled its way out. My team had won the National Championship!

I had stopped drinking after the baseball game and had just one shot to celebrate Duke's championship. My night was complete—at least I thought it was.

After partying for ten-plus hours, I was exhausted and ready to get some rest. I made the poor decision to drive myself home. On the way, I saw the worst thing imaginable: the red and blue lights of a police vehicle driving directly behind me, signaling me to pull over.

As I pulled over, so many thoughts were running through my mind. *What was I doing wrong? Stay calm; you've been through this before. I stopped drinking some time ago so he should not smell alcohol. Just remain calm, Jon.*

The officer stepped out of his vehicle and walked up to mine. He asked me for my license and registration, and I handed it over.

"I received a call that this vehicle has been swerving on the interstate," the officer said to me. "Have you been drinking?"

"Yes, officer, I did have some drinks today," I responded truthfully.

The officer had me step out of the vehicle to perform a field sobriety test, and surprisingly, I passed it.

But then his supervisor arrived on the scene, and the officer who had pulled me over told me quietly, "It's out of my hands now."

The supervisor insisted on performing another field sobriety test. I thought I did as well as before, but he told me I failed and would be arrested on a charge of Driving While Intoxicated

(DWI). The supervisor told me to turn around and place my hands behind my back. Once I was handcuffed and given my Miranda rights, he walked me to the squad car and drove me in to the station.

At the police station, he took my official Blood-Alcohol Content (BAC) level. It was over the legal limit, so I was booked on the DWI charge. Seventeen hours later, I was able to bail myself out. That was just the beginning of what seemed like a never-ending process with the courts. After about five months, I owned up completely and told my lawyer I just wanted it to be over. So, in August, I was sentenced to serve two years' probation and perform 30 hours of community service. I also was required to have an Interlock system installed in my car at my own expense. The device would make it impossible for me to operate my vehicle if I had consumed any alcohol.

Receiving my DWI was an eye-opening experience. It made me realize I could not continue living a life of partying and self-destruction. I needed to change. I just was not sure how to go about it. I did everything required by the judicial system, and I was so, *so* lucky: just two years of probation.

Now it was time for a big change in my life.

In the beginning of my new journey, it was difficult for me to hang out with my friends because all they wanted to do was drink. Legally, I could not do that anymore. I also knew I had been out of control, so it was time to stop anyway.

It took me a while, but I finally realized two things:

My friends needed to change, or,

I needed to change my friends.

That was hardest part of the journey for me. I had been enjoying life. For the first time, I was popular and having the time of my life. I had been feeling a high like I never felt before, because I had never before been considered popular. I did not want to lose the feeling.

While serving out my probation, I realized I wanted and needed more out of life. My dilemma was I didn't know how to accomplish it. As I continued my journey, I realized that if I wanted my life to change, I needed to first change myself.

Once I turned on that switch, magical things started occurring. I stopped blaming other people for what happened to me and I took ownership of my own life. And I realized everything that happens to you has a reason behind it.

Taking ownership of my life and problems caused me to look at things completely differently. I finally understood *I* was in complete control of my life and whether it was going to be good or bad rested squarely on my shoulders.

It is amazing how once you make a decision, everything starts to align. One night, I went to a social mixer and met someone named Ed Blunt. I did not realize that he was an entrepreneur, international speaker, trainer, and author. I definitely did not know at the time that he would alter the course of my life completely and forever. His energy was different from anyone I had ever met. I could feel that Mr. Blunt was different from most people. When he spoke, I became filled with life and positivity and it was uplifting.

As the night went on, I kept thinking to myself how amazing life could be if I could start to dream again. From that day forward, I created a new belief system. I began to share this new vision with my friends but they either did not see it or flat-out could not agree with my outlook on a new life. I decided it didn't matter as much as it would have earlier in my life. I knew this vision was given to me and only me. I began to realize that few people would understand, and I was willing to accept that.

In the beginning of my change, I lost people I thought were my friends. Now I realized they were just associates—people I hung out with because we had common ground.

As I started losing my existing friends, I started gaining new friends who were aligned with my new outlook on life. As I wanted more and needed more, I continued to exchange old friends for new friends who shared similar beliefs.

I started to expand my thinking. My head was filled with thoughts of positivity, goal setting, and reading and educating myself in the direction I desired to go. I focused more on personal development because I realized I had to become a better person. Once I became a better person, naturally I would become better in other aspects of life. So, I started reading books. Books on leadership, relationships, communication, thinking bigger, and being more efficient. In addition, I listened to audio recordings to further expose myself to new ways of thinking while commuting to and from work.

I often would listen to motivational speakers such as Johnny Wimbrey, Trent Shelton, Les Brown, Eric Thomas, Jim Rohn, Earl Nightingale, and the list goes on. I attended different seminars. I did everything I could to better myself. Until then, I never realized how many people wanted more out of life, just as I now did. It was a blessing to meet people who push you in the right direction—toward greatness. To be great, I realized I needed to be a student of the game.

If anyone were to ask me if I am successful, I would say, "Yes. I am successful because I have grown as a person. I communicate more efficiently and because of that, my relationship with people is better. I understand them better and I am more open to listening to their points of view."

And there is a lot more depth to my success as well, as I've learned a great deal about the power of thinking. Our dreams and thoughts take shape as a form of reality and what we focus on expands. As I've grown into leadership, I've realized one of the more important aspects is becoming the leader with dreams whom everyone wants to follow. I have been and am continuing to be mentored by leaders with powerful dreams, and I respect and emulate them.

As time passes and I connect with others, I pay the mentorship forward the way it was taught to me. I am currently working at Texas Live in Arlington, Texas, but I also work on my own personal business in the travel industry while I transition from employee to entrepreneur. I would love to tell you the rest of my story, but much like yours, my story is still being written.

I plan for the future, yet still live and cherish the precious moments in the now, just taking it one day at a time.

Biography

Jonathan Long wakes up every day hoping to inspire at least one person. He was born on November 21, 1985, in El Paso, Texas to Kevin and Fran Long. He graduated from South Hills High School in South Fort Worth, Texas, and then attended Tarrant County College for Communication Broadcasting in an effort to fulfill a childhood dream of becoming a disc jockey before electing to pursue another profession in the service industry. Long began his career in bartending because after being shy growing up, he developed a love for being around and interacting with people.

Jonathan is single and has no children.

He is currently transitioning from the service industry to entrepreneurship. While building his business is important and he has many goals in doing so, his ultimate goal in life is to serve, lead, and inspire others to reach and maximize their fullest potential as a person and in their careers. Jonathan plans to become a mentor to more people as his skills continue to develop.

One of the ways he improves his leadership skills and moves toward his goals is by speaking life and positivity into others.

Contact Information:

Email: JonathanTLong2004@gmail.com
Facebook: Jonathan Long
Instagram: Jonathan_T_Long